# Positive Pupil Management and Motivation

## A Secondary Teacher's Guide

# Eddie McNamara

**David Fulton Publishers**

London

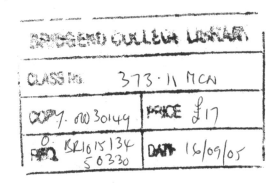
David Fulton Publishers Ltd
The Chiswick Centre, 414 Chiswick High Road, London W4 5TF
www.fultonpublishers.co.uk

First published in Great Britain in 1999 by David Fulton Publishers

Note: The rights of Eddie McNamara to be identified as the authors of this
work have been asserted by them in accordance with the Copyright, Designs
and Patents Act 1988.

David Fulton Publishers is a division of Granada Learning Limited, part of
Granada plc.

*British Library Cataloguing in Publication Data*
A catalogue record for this book is available from the British Library.

ISBN 1-85346-634-4

Typeset by Textype Typesetters, Cambridge
Printed and bound in Great Britain

# Contents

# CHAPTER 1

# Introduction

Difficult to manage adolescent behaviour is not a new phenomenon. Problems of youth have been of concern since early in man's history. For example Socrates wrote:

> Children now love luxury. They have bad manners, contempt for authority. They show disrespect for elders and love chatter in place of exercise: children are now tyrants not servants of their households.

Some authorities believe that challenging behaviour can be viewed as a characteristic of adolescence and that it is normal and to be expected. In 1988 a major inquiry into the subject was instigated by the Government under the chairmanship of Lord Elton. The report, known as the Elton Report on Discipline in Schools was published in 1989. At dissemination conferences the view was put forward that to aim to totally eliminate problematic pupils was unrealistic – a more realistic aim was to 'marginalise' the problem(s), i.e. to have effective school systems in place to respond to pupil misbehaviour so that problems of pupil discipline could be handled comfortably and not dominate the school's agenda.

The findings of the Elton Report can be summarised as follows:

- the causes of pupil problem behaviour are multiple and diverse; and consequently,
- the possible responses to such behaviour can be multiple and diverse.

This summary position is taken as the starting point for this book.

The identified causes of problem behaviour may:

- be predominantly *within the child* (e.g. emotional disturbance);
- be attributed to *home background* and *neighbourhood factors* (e.g. family stress);
- be due to *classroom factors* (e.g. seating arrangements, teacher management style);
- be contributed to by *school system factors* and *management decisions* (e.g. room allocation, incentive and sanction systems).

Frequently factors contributing to pupil problem behaviour reside in more than one of these four areas and may be interactive in nature. A model to represent this is presented in Figure 1.1.

*Home background* factors can be responded to by accommodation, compensation or communication. For example, the absence of suitable conditions for completing coursework at home can be accommodated or compensated for by allowing pupils to study in the school library before start of school, during lunchtime and after school. 'Disinterested' parents can be encouraged by efficient friendly communications from the school.

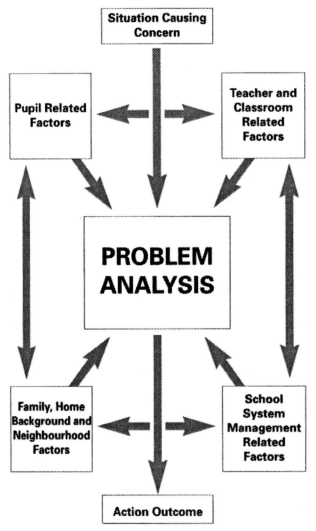

**Figure 1.1** Contributory factors to problem behaviour

*Pupil factors* can also be responded to in a variety of ways. For example, if pupils are disruptive because of a lack of social skills then social skills groupwork could be included in the personal and social education (PSE) curriculum; if a pupil is emotionally disturbed then pastoral counselling or counselling from support service personnel may be arranged; if solvent abuse is a problem then liaison with the community drugs team is required.

Thus while some of the contributory factors cannot be directly influenced or controlled by teachers (e.g. family stress), some factors can be directly controlled (e.g. by school policies and classroom management practices).

The most efficient use of teachers' skills and time is achieved by directing it at those factors over which they have most control and therefore can have most influence. These factors predominantly reside in the two boxes on the right hand side of the model in Figure 1.1 (McNamara 1990). Therefore in addition to an assessment of the nature of the pupil's problem behaviour, an assessment of context factors (i.e. within classroom and within school system factors) is a necessary prerequisite for a comprehensive assessment of problem behaviour in the school situation. This emphasis upon classroom and school system factors should not be interpreted as under-emphasising the significance of within pupil factors and family background factors but merely as an effective approach to the management of pupil behaviour which addresses in the first instance those contributory factors over which teachers have most direct control – for it is often a manipulation of context factors which constitutes the intervention of first choice.

## THE SCHOOL

Schools are complex systems and require effective management. This management can be viewed as operating at three levels, and for the management of pupil behaviour the levels can be described as:

Level 1: *Whole-School* pupil management policies and practices.

Level 2: *Classroom* management policies and practices.

Level 3: *Individual pupil* management policies and practices.

These levels are represented diagrammatically in Figure 1.2. Integrated, consistent, monitored and evaluated pupil management policies, permeating from level 1 through level 2 to level 3, are the hallmarks of the effective school.

Sometimes assessment of pupil behaviour at level 3 reveals policy or practice shortcomings at level 2 and/or level 1. If level 2 and/or level 1 policy or practice shortcomings or deficits contribute to level 3 problems, then to restrict the

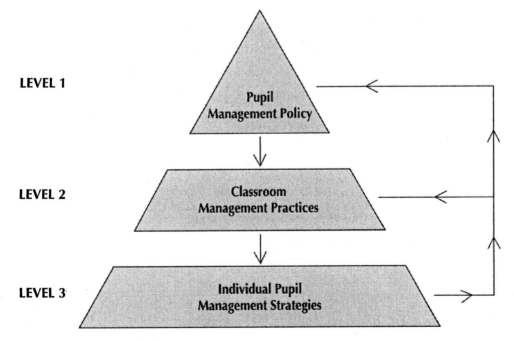

**Figure 1.2** 'Levels' of intervention

intervention to level 3 would at best resolve a problem for the time being but not contribute to a preventive approach – achieved by intervening at level 2 and/or level 1. Intervention at levels 1 or 2 would reduce the probability of similar problems occurring in the future. At worst, not addressing level 2 or level 1 contributory factors to level 3 problems is to accept a status quo that should not be accepted: in the extreme it could result in the consequences of school management shortcomings being erroneously interpreted as 'pupil problems'. The following two examples are of level 3 'problems' which are more appropriately addressed at level 2 or level 1.

*Problem pupil behaviour more appropriately addressed at level 2 (classroom)*
Kevin was referred to a Behaviour Support Team because of disruptive behaviour in class. Classroom observation data (Jolly and McNamara 1992) revealed that Kevin's level of on-task behaviour was very similar to the class average. Kevin was on task for an average of 65 per cent of the time and the class average was 69 per cent. Scrutiny of the data also revealed that five pupils in the teaching group were on task for less time than Kevin.

This data supported the Behaviour Support Team members' judgement that a whole class (level 2) intervention was more appropriate than a level 1 (individual pupil) intervention.

*Problem pupil behaviour more appropriately addressed at level 1 (school policy)*
Class 10.8, the eighth set of an eight class year group, was referred to a Behaviour Support Team because of disruptive behaviour during English lessons. Classroom observation (narrative account) revealed that in a number of lessons the task was for each pupil to read aloud in turn from their personal copy of *Lord of the Flies*. The text was assessed for Readability Level and this was found to be in the range 14.0 years to 14 years 10 months. The reading competence of the pupils was assessed and found to range from 9 years 3 months to 12 years 11 months with the average being 12 years 3 months (London Reading Test).

The Behaviour Support Team members did not recommend a classroom pupil management programme: it was suggested that the English Department review the pupil–curriculum demand 'match' and that the teaching methodology be reviewed. This response is level 1 (school policy) and can be viewed as a preventive response.

The chapters that follow contain descriptions of strategies for the management of problem pupil behaviour. The strategies are presented at the levels of:

- whole class interventions
- individual pupil interventions.

Implicit in the rationale of intervention are the assumptions that (a) for each level of problem analysis, consideration has been given to whether 'higher level' factors contribute to the presenting problems, and, if so, (b) that the identified higher level contributory factors have been addressed.

CHAPTER 2

# Classroom management

The aims of this chapter are to:

- Illustrate the place of classroom management within a whole school approach to pupil management.
- Describe the theory of pupil management.
- In the context of pupil management, describe the need for
  - rules of the classroom
  - pupil involvement
  - feedback to pupils
  - responses to inappropriate behaviour
  - evaluative statements.

The interventions described have been implemented successfully in schools and therefore have 'chalk face' validity. However the interventions have even greater power and utility when the rationale underlying them is explicit and understood. When this is the case the user has greater flexibility and diversity of approach, as appreciation of the principles that generate the interventions creates the potential for many different management interventions to be generated. This consideration is the reason for presenting the rationale underlying the intervention, i.e. why the management practices are suggested and why they 'work'.

## CLASSROOM MANAGEMENT – THE THEORY

### Antecedents–Behaviour–Consequences (A-B-C)

The A-B-C statement of the relationship between behaviour and its antecedents and consequences is central to the analysis and management of pupil behaviour.

The A-B-C model is used to generate classroom management interventions. The model is the central conceptual statement of the relationship of behaviour (B) to the environment. Environmental factors can be sorted into those which precede the behaviour, the antecedents (A) and those which follow the behaviour, the consequences (C). The 'laws' of behaviour underpinning this model are:

- *Behaviour* is influenced by its consequences – the B-C dimension. Behaviour which is followed by something nice, *positive reinforcement*, increases in frequency. Behaviour which is followed by something not nice, *punishment*, is suppressed. Behaviour which has its reinforcer withdrawn is extinguished.
- To *change behaviour* by positive reinforcement requires the behaviour to be reinforced immediately, frequently and consistently.

● To *maintain behaviour* at a high frequency requires the behaviour to be reinforced intermittently.

### Antecedents

*The probability of behaviour occurring is influenced by its antecedents* – the A-B dimension. In education settings the antecedents to behaviour can be considered under four headings:

● *Stimulus conditions* – the immediate precursors to pupil behaviour (e.g. teacher–pupil interaction).
● *Setting factors* (e.g. desk arrangements, publicly posted rules).
● *Curriculum* (e.g. content, structure and delivery).
● *Organisational factors* (e.g. incentive and sanctions systems, mixed ability/streamed classes). See Figure 2.1.

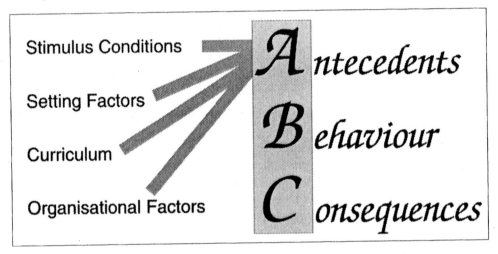

**Figure 2.1** The relationship of Antecedents to behaviour in the classroom

### Behaviour

The main concern of teachers when faced with the management of a difficult pupil or class of pupils is the actual behaviour of the pupil(s). Consequently the focus of the concern is pupil behaviour – the B of the A-B-C model.

### Consequences

Behaviour is influenced by its consequences. Teacher response to pupil behaviour is a significant consequence of pupil behaviour in classroom situations, i.e. teacher response to pupil behaviour is a powerful determinant of that behaviour. There are a range of teacher responses, both verbal and non-verbal, which can influence pupil behaviour – the most significant being:

● teacher praise (positive feedback)
● teacher criticism (negative feedback) in response to pupil appropriate/ inappropriate social and academic behaviour.

In summary, in addition to consequences, the other major determinants of behaviour are the immediate antecedents of the behaviour, i.e. what happens immediately before (stimulus conditions); the classroom situation (setting factors); what is being asked of the pupils (curriculum content, structure and delivery), and organisational factors such as the composition of the class (e.g. mixed ability or set). Thus if pupil behaviour (B), its antecedents (A), and significant consequences (C) are assessed, an analysis of pupil behaviour can be pursued. This is known as a functional analysis.

## Functional analysis

Teachers can use their own professional judgements to carry out a functional analysis or they may arrange for a teacher colleague to observe the classroom situation, activities and interactions. The situation may warrant a particularly rigorous observational assessment using classroom situation, pupil management and pupil behaviour schedules such as those described in Jolly and McNamara (1992).

Pupil behaviour of concern to teachers lies between functional antecedents and consequences – these antecedents and consequences give the behaviour meaning and allow an analysis of its function or purpose to be pursued – for behaviour has both *structure and function.* The 'structure' is the actual behaviour while the 'function' is the purpose the behaviour serves. For example, if a pupil calls out 'help!' (structure) in a classroom, does he or she want help (function) with an academic task? Does the pupil wish the teacher to intervene (function) because he or she is being assaulted by another pupil? If a pupil runs out (structure) of the classroom, is he or she [suffer]ing from diarrhoea and heading for the toilet (function)? Is he or she escap[ing] from teacher criticism (function)? The actual behaviours often tell us little ab[o]ut its function. Function is determined by an analysis of *context factors.* Func[tio]nal analysis is the term used to describe this analysis. For example, teacher a[tte]ntion can be obtained by any of the following pupil behaviours: raising a han[d a]nd waiting quietly, completing all the set work, calling out, leaving seat, tapping [a] pencil on the desk. Such a range of different behaviours which serve the sa[me] function is known as a functional response class and gives rise in turn to [the] concept of a functional response class hierarchy. The new hierarchy [is u]sed to describe the fact that the probability of a pupil engaging in a specific [beh]aviour will vary according to the 'strength' of the behaviour-consequence rela[tio]nship, i.e. whether the behaviour will achieve the intended outcome.

A number of [different] types of [at]tention seeking behaviour are listed above and the strength of each ['behaviour-co]nsequence' relationship depends on the history of success of the behaviour [in ac]hieving the desired consequence. For example, if a pupil is regularly attended to by the teacher in the English lesson when he or she raises their hand, then the 'strength' of 'raising hand' behaviour is enhanced; conversely if in the French lesson 'raising hand' behaviour is not attended to then the 'strength' of this behaviour (in this setting) will be reduced – and perhaps the strength of other less appropriate pupil behaviours, e.g. shouting out, will be enhanced if they are attended to. Recognition and identification of relative hierarchical strengths within a pupil functional response class can therefore be helpful in leading to a more accurate problem analysis and effective intervention.

In summary, if a pupil gets more teacher attention by shouting out than by raising their hand then the pupil is more likely to shout for teacher attention than to raise their hand. This has obvious implications for an intervention programme, for the effectiveness of the two behaviours would have to be interchanged for raising hand behaviour to be 'stronger' than shouting out behaviour and therefore be the pupil's preferred behaviour for gaining teacher attention.

Sometimes it is not possible to identify the reinforcer(s) that sustain disruptive behaviour(s), i.e. the function. In such circumstances it may be necessary to implement a management programme that 'swamps' or overrides the effect of the unidentified reinforcers of the disruptive behaviour.

## Situation analysis

Situational factors can enhance or reduce the strength of the A-B (Antecedent–Behaviour) and B-C (Behaviour–Consequence) relationships. For example, the liklihood of 'raising hand' behaviour will be increased if the teacher prefaces a question to the class with the reminder 'remember to put your hand up if you know the answer'. The teacher's statement (i.e. the reminder) is a setting factor and the actual question put to the class is the eliciting stimulus – both of which promote the probability of 'raising hand' behaviour.

A context factor which will strengthen or weaken the strength of the A-B relationship is general classroom discipline. If the behaviour of the class is noisy and unruly, then the effectiveness of the cue 'remember to raise your hand if you know the answer' in promoting 'raising hand' behaviour will be diminished: if the behaviour of the class is quiet and task orientated then the effectiveness of the cue in promoting 'raising hand' behaviour will be enhanced.

If 'raising hand' behaviour is recognised by the teacher then the strength of the B ('raising hand')–C (teacher recognition) relationship is increased. A context factor which would further strengthen the B-C relationship is a classroom environment that allows other pupils to perceive the B-C relationship, i.e. an orderly classroom that allows a teacher to make a comment such as 'good to see so many of you with your hands up. John, how would you tackle this problem . . .?' Conversely a classroom situation in which there is lots of inappropriate behaviour and lack of attention paid to the teacher will have the effect of diminishing the strength of the B-C relationship – for the 'connection' between the 'raising hand' behaviour and the teacher response (recognition of appropriate hand raising behaviour and specific recognition of John) will be 'missed' by the majority of the pupils as they will not be paying attention to the lesson. Therefore, in addition to the observation of pupil classroom behaviour, it is important to observe situation factors which may influence the occurrence of appropriate and inappropriate pupil behaviour.

There are many situation factors in school settings which have the potential to influence pupil behaviour. In 1988 Alessi listed ten situational factors which he judged to be significant and which should be considered when assessing the context of pupil behaviour. They are:

1. Pupil grouping arrangements.
2. Grouping levels, i.e. pupil/curriculum difficulty match.
3. Seating arrangements.
4. Teacher–directed versus project work and pace of lesson.
5. Instructional format.
6. Subject area.
7. Lesson transition, rules and routines.
8. Physical arrangement and organisation of the classroom.
9. Timetable planning and student management practices.
10. Choices, i.e. are pupils given choices and responsibility and are management practices in place to assure pupils are taught to accept this responsibility?

A rigorous analysis of the classroom situation can be carried out using the Classroom Situation Checklist (in Jolly and McNamara 1992). This can be used by a class teacher for Teacher Self-Assessment or by a support service teacher or departmental colleague for independent assessments. This checklist facilitates an assessment of some of the more immediate antecedent determinants of pupil behaviour.

## System analysis

Secondary schools are complex organisations which require many management decisions to be made both at the policy and implementation levels. Decisions made at the systems level may influence pupil behaviour either directly or indirectly via situational or context factors. The following example illustrates this. A class may have to move between two classrooms for a lesson change – Geography may be taught in a room at the top of one teaching block and Spanish (the next lesson) may be taught in a different teaching block. If a bell signals the end of one lesson and the beginning of the next then it is physically impossible for the Spanish lesson to start on time in a brisk, orderly fashion. Thus context factors, e.g. the teachers having to repeat instructions for late-comers, may be the antecendents for inappropriate pupil behaviour: some pupils may become bored at the lesson not progressing and therefore engage in less appropriate behaviour. This is illustrative of how a system factor can serve to weaken the strength of the Antecedent–Behaviour–Consequence sequences which are compatible with orderly pupil behaviour and academic progression. A rigorous analysis of school systems is outside the scope of this book but an awareness of the potential influence of such factors will enhance the insightfullness of problem analysis.

A model to represent the way in which simple A-B-C relationships are 'nested' in context factors – which in turn may be 'nested' in system factors – is presented in Figure 2.2.

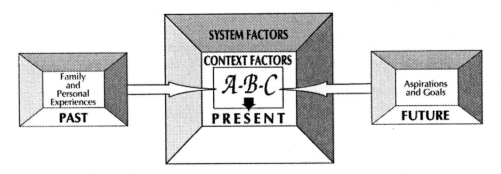

**Figure 2.2** Antecedents–Behaviour–Consequences: the relationship with context and systems

A current movement in some secondary schools is towards the development of Peer Support Groups. A Peer Support Group is a self-help, school based group, which, through a philosophy of sharing and mutual support, help each other and other colleagues to respond more effectively to problems of pupil management. Such an activity is increased in effectiveness when group members operate within a functional, situational and systems analysis.

In summary, there is a two-pronged approach to addressing issues of pupil behaviour – preventive proactive approaches and reactive approaches. The relationship of the two approaches to the A-B-C model is illustrated in Figure 2.3.

It is, however, important to note that classroom management strategies based on the manipulation of consequences of behaviour (behaviour modification) have been criticised: in particular, the criticism has been made that the use of behaviour modification can be unethical – for the techniques of behaviour modification can be used to sustain an educational status quo that should not be supported, e.g. 'Behaviour Modification in the Classroom: Sit Down: Be Quiet: Be Docile' (Winett and Winkler 1972). Such criticism has the potential to be valid: it is therefore of the utmost importance that the curriculum materials available in the classroom are relevant, appropriately differentiated, structured and delivered in a manner that achieves appropriate task/pupil ability match. This ensures that 'understandable' pupil disinterest and disengagement from inappropriate curriculum materials is not inadvertently and inappropriately interpreted as indicating that inappropriate pupil behaviour is the primary problem. In such a situation the inappropriate curriculum content/structure/delivery is the primary problem to be addressed – the pupil behaviour is at best a secondary problem and perhaps not a problem that can be 'accepted' until the primary problems have been addressed.

## CLASSROOM MANAGEMENT – THE PRACTICE

Pupil management practices looked at in the context of the A-B-C model are referred to as behavioural approaches because they focus on pupil behaviour. Since the late 1960s many research reports have appeared demonstrating the effectiveness of behavioural approaches in improving pupil behaviour in

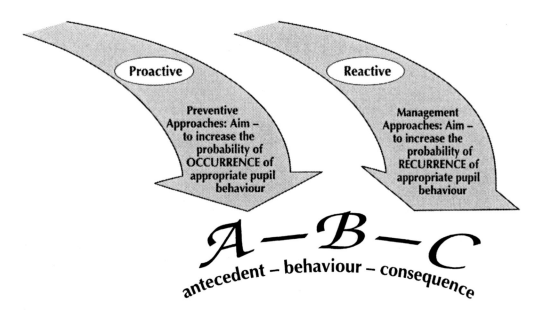

**Figure 2.3** Preventive and reactive approaches to problem behaviour: Relationship with Antecedents–Behaviour–Consequences model

classrooms. One of the earliest reports was that of Madsen *et al.* (1968). The authors reported how the use of 'rules, praise and ignore' significantly improved the classroom behaviour of primary-aged pupils. Similar positive outcomes were subsequently reported with older, secondary-aged pupils, e.g. McAllister *et al.* (1969). Helpful books on classroom management then began to appear, e.g. *Behaviour Modification for the Classroom Teacher* (Axelrod 1977), *Behaviour Modification in the Classroom* (Harrop, 1983).

In more recent years substantial, effective INSET (In Service Education for Teachers) resources have been made available commercially, e.g. *Preventive Approaches to Disruption* (Chisholme *et al.* 1986), *Building a Better Behaved School* (Galvin *et al.* 1990).

Of the wide ranging aspects of classroom management described in these research papers, books and resource packs, central, pervasive and persuasive is the need for behavioural standards of classroom behaviour to be made explicit, usually in the form of rules of the classroom.

## Rules of the classroom

Rules make known explicitly to pupils the implicit expectations of teachers concerning pupil behaviour. Rules, clearly defined and made explicit, negate the need to pursue sterile discussion and debate around assertions such as 'pupils should know how to behave' and 'pupils should know the rules of the classroom'.

## Rules about rules

There are a few rules about rules. Rules should:

- be few in number
- be simple
- be described positively
- reflect the concerns of the teachers
- be consistent with the school pupil management policy.

They should be few in number because it is more likely they will be remembered.

They should be simple so that it is more likely they will be understood.

They should be described positively so that the teacher will then focus on positive pupil management strategies.

They should reflect the concerns of the teachers as they will more likely be relevant to the particular teaching situation.

They should be consistent with the school pupil management policy so that they contribute to an overall whole school consistent approach to promoting appropriate pupil behaviour.

### *A cautionary note*

It must be remembered that rules themselves will probably not influence pupil behaviour. If pupils are motivated to conform to school/teachers' requirements, then a knowledge of 'expected behaviour' facilitates pupil self-regulation. However, for large numbers of pupils the existence of rules may not influence pupil behaviour. This is because a major determinant of behaviour is the immediate consequence. If pupils comply with the rules of the classroom and no positive consequences follow, e.g. teacher recognition, then the likelihood of future rule compliance is less than if the converse was the case. Similarly, if pupils breach the rules of the classroom and no negative consequence follows, then the likelihood of future breaches of the classroom rules remains.

The formulation of classroom rules and giving them a 'high profile' may have an unforeseen, undesirable consequence. The existence of rules may have the undesirable consequence of increasing the level of teacher negative, coercive behaviour, i.e. telling pupils off and threatening pupils with sanctions. This is because the existence of rules may sensitise the teacher to breaches of the rules, which may in turn encourage teachers to be more negative towards the pupils.

For this reason rules being followed should always be recognised in a positive manner. When initially introduced and while the pupils are learning to follow the classroom rules the 'rule following behaviour' should be recognised in a positive fashion immediately, frequently and consistently. Over time, as rule compliance becomes the classroom norm, rule following behaviour should be recognised positively but intermittently, i.e. now and again during the course of the lesson.

These two schedules of reinforcement will maximise the likelihood of rule following behaviour being acquired and maintained by pupils.

*The criticism trap.* Most pupils will comply in the short term when told to 'sit down', 'be quiet', 'get on with your work' and so on. Such an immediate response often encourages the teacher to tell pupils off more frequently because the management strategy appears 'to work': technically it can be said that the teacher has been negatively reinforced for telling pupils off – for an aversive consequence (pupil misbehaviour) has been removed. However, research indicates, e.g. Becker *et al.* (1975), that when such an approach is the only management practice used, the problem behaviour often increases in frequency. Thus, while there is an immediate cessation of the behaviour, in a longer time frame the behaviour occurs more frequently. This analysis explains why some teachers persist in using negative control techniques when they patently 'don't work'. This is not to say that pupil attention should not be drawn to the fact that the pupil is misbehaving: rather, such teacher behaviour should be embedded in a predominantly positive teacher management regime, e.g. an observer in the classroom should be able to record up to four positive teacher/pupil interactions to every negative interaction.

## Rule formulation

Teacher responses to the following prompts will facilitate the identification of appropriate and relevant classroom rules:

(i)     identify the pupil behaviour(s) you want to see more of;
(ii)    identify the pupil behaviour(s) you want to see less of.

Can you think of a rule that will encourage (i) above while at the same time discourage (ii) above?

For example, pupil 'shouting out' behaviour may be identified as a particularly disruptive behaviour which should at least be reduced, and preferably extinguished. At the same time 'hand raising behaviour' (for a pupil to contribute to the lesson) may be a behaviour that the teacher wishes to encourage and see more of. Therefore, a rule 'Wait to be called upon to contribute to the lesson' will probably facilitate a reduction in 'calling out' behaviour and may also help to promote 'hand raising' behaviour. However, the likelihood of promoting 'hand raising behaviour' is further increased if the specific desired behaviour is made explicit in the rule. Therefore the following rule will probably be more effective in promoting hand raising behaviour, 'Raise your hand and wait to be called before answering or speaking'.

The following will facilitate a self-check of rules of the classroom:

- What are the rules of your classroom?
- Were the pupils involved in rule formulation?
- What strategies do you use to promote rule compliance?
- What strategies do you employ to use the rules of the classroom to redirect inappropriate pupil behaviour?
- What strategies do you employ to ensure you do not get caught in the 'criticism trap' (see above)?

The emphasis on the need for rules makes no assumptions about what are appropriate and inappropriate classroom behaviours. Decisions in this area are the responsibility of the classroom teacher, often in consultation with departmental and other school colleagues. For example, some teachers require a silent classroom with oral contributions 'allowed' only when a pupil is called on by the teacher: other teachers allow pupil to pupil talk during written work assignments and so on.

The cardinal principle is that the teacher must be explicit about appropriate and inappropriate pupil behaviour – and this information must be made known to the pupils in the form of rules of the classroom.

### Teacher dominant–pupil submissive model of pupil management

The traditional model of classroom control incorporates the teacher as controller and the pupils as controlled, i.e. the teacher directs and the pupil is directed. Implicit in this model is the assumption that the teacher is dominant and the pupil is submissive.

However, there is inherent potential for stress, tension and conflict in this model – for the possibility always exists that the submissive party, namely the pupil, may choose not to be submissive. When this is the case, i.e. when the pupil(s) chooses not to be submissive, conflict can result, as the pupil may be seen to be challenging the authority of the teacher. In contrast to this 'dominant–submissive' orientated model, the cooperative learning model circumvents this potential for conflict – for the model is based on an assumption of teachers and pupils as partners.

Within the cooperative model the teacher and pupil agree standards of behaviour, academic targets, assessment of behaviour and academic achievements and so on. Agreements can even be arrived at as to ways of recognising and rewarding achievement and ways of addressing 'problems' when standards of behaviour are not achieved or academic targets not reached. The teacher's role in these processes is that of facilitator: the teacher does not take personal exception to rule transgressions but merely ensures that the agreed consequences come into effect, and the teacher is also available to help the pupil plan future courses of action to avoid replication of the transgressions. The situation is perhaps best compared to that of a football team: for the teacher and pupil are both kicking towards the same (agreed) goal. Scoring a goal is then an occasion for mutual celebration: conceding a goal is an occasion for a review of tactics, exhortation to increased effort and monitoring of future performance. (Further relevant reading on this area of education can be found in Glasser (1990) – a book which addresses the issues of managing students without coercion.)

### Pupil involvement in rule formulation

The *imposition* of rules of behaviour on a class of pupils holds the intrinsic potential for conflict: this is because the inherent underlying model of pupil management adheres to the teacher dominant/pupil submissive model. For this reason it is preferable that the pupils are involved in rule formulation.

If the pupils are actively involved in rule formulation then the likelihood of the pupils 'owning' the rules is enhanced. 'Owning' in this context means 'identifying with and accepting'. When such ownership exists, not only is pupil rule compliance more likely, but pupil acceptance of sanctions for non rule compliance is promoted, i.e. the likelihood of a pupil responding to a sanction with aggression, defiance or other non accepting behaviour is reduced.

However, it may be the case that the classroom order and control necessary to involve pupils in the formulation of rules is very difficult to achieve because of the very fact that the class of pupils is disruptive. In such a situation the rules have to be imposed on the class of pupils. When this is the case pupil acceptance and 'ownership' can be retrospectively promoted by involving the class of pupils in discussing, reviewing and if necessary modifying the classroom rules when the level of appropriate pupil classroom behaviour permits.

### The use of rules to redirect pupil behaviour

The imposition of authority by a teacher to redirect pupil behaviour is fraught with potential difficulties. In particular, the possibility always exists that the problem situation can become worse because of escalation of pupil problem behaviour as described above.

By contrast, the public posting of 'rules of the classroom' can:

- facilitate the redirection of inappropriate pupil behaviour;
- achieve this redirection in an effective, depersonalised low-key manner.

The public posting of rules enables the teacher to redirect pupil behaviour by drawing the pupil's attention to the relevant rule, e.g. 'John, the rule is "put your hand up if you want to answer the question"'. This is a 'neutral' method of redirecting pupil behaviour and contrasts with a personalised teacher intervention such as, 'John, I told you not to shout out'.

In addition, the public posting of rules facilitates subtle redirection of pupil behaviour. For example, a pupil may be misbehaving and the teacher, having made eye contact with the pupil, may merely point to the list of rules on display. Subsequent pupil on-task behaviour could then be positively reinforced with a smile, or at 'thumbs up' sign.

### Pupil self-assessment of rule compliance

Pupil self-assessment is an integral part of any pupil self-management programme and is considered in Chapters 3, 4 and 5. However, a pupil self-assessment component can be incorporated into a substantially teacher determined classroom management programme. This is achieved as follows.

- The rules of the classroom are determined in a manner consistent with the considerations described above. The pupils are then asked to copy the rules into the back of their classbook and to make a self-assessment pro-forma as illustrated in Figure 2.4.
- At the beginning of each lesson the pupils are:
  - reminded of the rules of the classroom

- informed that at the end of the lesson they will be asked to judge if they have substantially followed each rule throughout the course of the lesson.
- If they have, they are to tick the appropriate rule. If they have not, they are to put a cross next to the rule.
- In addition, in order to encourage accurate self-assessment, the teacher 'marks' the pupils' self-assessment.
- For pupils who have followed the rules and self-assessed accurately, teacher positive comments can reflect both accuracy of self-assessment and the fact of rule following behaviour.
- For pupils who have not complied fully with the rules and have acknowledged the fact by accurate self-assessment, the honesty and accuracy of self-assessment can be acknowledged – together with an 'invitation' to focus on rule following behaviour with respect to particular rule(s) during the next lesson.
- With pupils who have not engaged in rule following behaviour but self-assessed as if they had, discussion with the pupil would focus on
  - whether the pupil honestly believes that they have been engaged in rule following behaviour when he or she has not, or
  - whether the pupil has not taken the task of self-assessing rule compliance seriously.

It may be more appropriate for a card or booklet to be the 'software' for pupil self-assessment of rule compliance. Such a card or booklet could be used for a particular lesson (e.g. History) in which the behaviour of a significant number of pupils was problematic. If pupil behaviour in a number of different curriculum areas was of particular concern, then the practice of rule compliance self-assessment could be extended to all lessons. Examples of rule compliance self-assessment protocols are illustrated in Chapter 3.

| RULE | LESSON | | | | | | |
|---|---|---|---|---|---|---|---|
| | 1 | 2 | 3 | 4 | 5 | 6 | 7 |
| 1. Arrive on time | ✔ | ✔ | ✘ | ✔ | ✔ | ✔ | ✘ |
| 2. Complete work | ✔ | ✔ | ✘ | ✔ | ✔ | ✔ | ✔ |
| 3. No "put-downs" | ✔ | ✔ | ✔ | ✔ | ✘ | ✔ | ✔ |
| 4. Work quietly | ✔ | ✔ | ✔ | ✔ | ✔ | ✔ | ✘ |

**Figure 2.4** Self-assessment: rule compliance

## Feedback

Feedback is the term used to describe the transmission of information about performance to the performer. Feedback is an essential requirement for adaptive behaviour – for knowledge of outcome of behaviour can be compared with intended outcome. This comparison subsequently provides information which determines future performance.

If actual behaviour and intended behaviour are in agreement, this information confirms previous performance which is likely to be repeated in similar circumstances. If actual behaviour and intended behaviour are not in agreement, this information can be used to vary subsequent performance in an effort to achieve congruence (see Chapter 5).

There are *two components to feedback*: these are information and reinforcement.

- The *information* component helps self-monitoring and self-evaluation of performance to occur in the manner described above.
- The *reinforcing* component increases the likelihood of the behaviour being repeated.

The potential of information feedback, to promote pupil self-regulation of behaviour change, is harnessed in pupil self-management programmes: these programmes can be targeted at whole classes of pupils.

The positive *reinforcement potential* of feedback has been utilised by teachers for many years to encourage and promote appropriate pupil behaviour. The introduction of behaviour modification techniques into the classroom management practices of teachers, structured and further promoted the 'normal' positive encouragement of appropriate pupil behaviour by teachers. This structuring and consequent increased effectiveness of pupil management by teachers has been achieved by using the techniques of behaviour modification to encourage pupils to behave appropriately.

*Behaviour modification* is based on the assumption that pupil behaviour is substantially determined by its consequences. Behaviour that is followed by a *rewarding consequence* is more likely to recur. Therefore one of the tasks of a teacher is to arrange for appropriate pupil behaviour to be followed by rewarding consequences e.g. teacher attention..

Behaviour that has its *reinforcer removed* extinguishes, i.e. 'goes away'. In reality, when the reinforcer of a behaviour is removed, the behaviour sometimes increases in frequency and/or intensity of occurrence – only if the reinforcement is still withheld does the behaviour eventually extinguish. Therefore a second task of a teacher is to identify if inappropriate pupil behaviour is being inadvertently reinforced by a positive consequence occurring in the classroom: if this is the case, the teacher should arrange for the reinforcement to follow appropriate behaviour – thereby bringing about the extinction of inappropriate behaviour and the substitution of the inappropriate behaviour by appropriate behaviour.

Behaviour that is *followed by a punishment* is suppressed: when the punishment or the threat of punishment is removed, the behaviour will return – probably at its former level and possibly at a more intense level.

When *new behaviours* are being learnt or when a desired behaviour occurs infrequently, then the acquisition of new behaviour and/or the increased frequency of occurrence of behaviour are promoted by following the schedule of reinforcement:

- reinforce *immediately*
- reinforce *consistently*
- reinforce *frequently.*

The above rationale and guidance for teachers to modify and change pupil behaviour in pro-social and pro-academic directions, are couched in psychological terms which may not immediately bring to mind examples of real-life teacher behaviour. Some examples of teacher positive and negative behaviours are listed below: these may function as positive and negative reinforcement (or punishment) to effect change in pupil behaviour.

## Teacher positive feedback

*Non-verbal reinforcers*
- Eye contact and 'friendly' expression.
- Standing close to pupil, nodding while scrutinising work.
- 'Thumbs up' sign or other esoteric signal.
- A variety of facial expressions which are open, non-threatening and friendly.

*Verbal reinforcers*
- Single word comments which are received as *praise* by the pupils, e.g. 'spot on', 'great', 'excellent', 'correct', 'right'.
- Sentences *specifying the appropriate behaviours* that are being recognised and encouraged, e.g. 'Well presented work, John', 'Michael, you've been working very quietly, keep it up', 'Edward, thank you for helping Rachael'.
- *Personalised positive comments* – these are more effective reinforcers of behaviour than vaguely directed comments, i.e. use the pupil's name.
- Engage in a conversation with a pupil about non-work related matters, i.e. *show an interest* in the pupil as a person.
- *Offering help* or inquiring if help is required in a pleasant tone of voice.
- Calling on pupils in class by using *positive descriptive phrases*, e.g. 'George looks as if he knows the answer', 'John has his hand up, I think I'll ask him'.

*Written reinforcers*
- *Positive, personalised comments* in exercise books, e.g. 'Good work, John', 'Excellent effort, Michael', 'Nice try, Jim'.
- By regular *letters home* or comments in *home–school log book or homework diary* communicating information about good work or good behaviour in school.

*Written positive reinforcement* has advantages over verbal and non-verbal positive reinforcers. Verbal and non-verbal reinforcers act at the time they are used, i.e. while their effect on pupil behaviour may have some permanence, the actual reinforcement has an effect only at the time it is delivered. In contrast, written reinforcers may have an effect, i.e. a positive reinforcing effect, each time they are read by the pupil. *A written positive reinforcement has the potential to have a repeated effect.*

A second advantage of written reinforcement over verbal reinforcement is that it can be combined with diagnostic marking. This is written feedback which indicates how performance can be further improved, e.g. 'John, seven out of ten. Good. The work could be further improved by . . .'

Written reinforcement – as verbal and non-verbal reinforcement – is increased in effectiveness if it is personalised (ie the pupil's first name is written down to emphasise the personal nature of the communication).

## Teacher negative feedback

Negative feedback is similar to positive feedback in that the performer receives information about performance: but positive feedback contains information about the correctness of performance whereas negative feedback informs the performer that the performance is, for example, incorrect, wrong, inaccurate, undesirable

Negative feedback is different from positive feedback in that positive feedback has a positive reinforcement component, whereas negative feedback may have a punishment component.

In a particular feedback situation it is impossible to specify precisely, in a quantitative manner, the relative loading of information and positive reinforcement or punishment. However, it is possible to make judgements about the relative loadings as the following examples illustrate.

- *'That's wrong, John'*, said in a quiet, friendly voice. This negative feedback would have a high negative feedback informational loading and a low, perhaps negligible, negative feedback punishment loading.
- *'That's wrong, John'*, shouted across the classroom in an angry, irritated tone of voice, would have a high negative feedback informational loading and a high negative feedback punishment loading.
- *'That answer is correct, John'*, said in a friendly tone of voice. This positive feedback would have a high positive feedback informational loading and a significant positive reinforcement loading.
- *'Great, well done. That answer is correct, John'*, said in a friendly tone of voice. This positive feedback would have a high positive feedback informational loading and a high positive reinforcement loading.

These examples of positive and negative feedback are illustrated in Figure 2.5.

When considering the inappropriate/undesirable behaviour it is crucial that the alternative appropriate/desirable behaviour is considered as well. Since pupils cannot engage in both appropriate and inappropriate behaviour at the same time the teacher will have two approaches to pursue in effecting pupil behaviour change: the teacher will aim to weaken the inappropriate behaviour while at the same time aim to strengthen the incompatible appropriate behaviour.

## Response strategies to inappropriate behaviour

- *Ignore.* It is sometimes preferable to ignore inappropriate behaviour rather than attend to it. Such a response however requires a number of qualifications:
  - The behaviour in question should be unobtrusive, e.g. day dreaming. If the behaviour is intrusive, i.e. obvious, public, disruptive, to ignore it would be contra indicated as it . . . would reduce the effectiveness of pupil learning and teacher

| TEACHER | DELIVERY | FEEDBACK CONTENT | | |
| --- | --- | --- | --- | --- |
| | | Information | Reward (motivational) | Punishment |
| i) 'that's wrong John' | quiet, friendly voice | high | possibly motivational | low/ negligible |
| ii) 'that's wrong John' | shouted across classroom, in an angry, irritated tone | high | none | high |
| iii) 'that answer is correct, John' | quiet, friendly tone of voice | high | high (motivational) | none |
| iv) 'great, well done: that answer is correct, John' | friendly tone of voice | high | very high (motivational) | none |

**Figure 2.5** The informational and incentive/sanction content of teacher feedback

teaching . . . perhaps indicate to the pupil in question and other pupils that the behaviour was acceptable and . . . reduce the influence of the rule indicating the alternative appropriate behaviour.
– The alternative appropriate behaviour(s) should be encouraged so as to progressively replace the inappropriate behaviour(s).
– The inappropriate behaviour should not be reinforced and therefore maintained by reinforcer(s) outside the teachers control, e.g. by the attention given to it by other pupils.

● *Punish*. Punishment has been defined earlier as a consequence that follows a behaviour and which has the effect of suppressing that behaviour. Sometimes the term 'punishment' conjures up thoughts of physical punishment, but in the context of pupil management it merely refers to an aversive consequence that the pupil 'doesn't like' and therefore which will suppress the behaviour it follows, e.g. a frown or a shake of the head could constitute an aversive consequence.

It is important to depersonalise the teacher–pupil interaction. For example, 'John, I told you to sit down' indicates the desired behaviour, i.e. (sitting down). However the 'I told you' content personalises the command: implicit in the command is the message 'I am the teacher and I told you to sit down'. The direction can be readily depersonalised by making reference to the appropriate classroom rule. For example the teacher could say, 'John, the classroom rule is "we sit at our desks to work" '. Should John not comply, then a direct challenge to the teacher's authority has been avoided: the further interaction between teacher and pupil revolves around following/not following rules, not around teacher authority.

- *Warning cues* – these are the least intrusive punishments and are a 'message' that the behaviour is inappropriate and should cease. Warning cues are preferably non-verbal, as verbal 'warnings' can be disruptive and distract other pupils in the class. Examples of non-verbal cues include physical proximity (going towards and standing near to the misbehaving pupil), eye contact (staring at the misbehaving pupil until the misbehaviour ceases), making eye contact with the pupil and indicating disapproval with a shake of the head. If compliance occurs it is important to ensure that social reinforcement follows a little after the pupil returns to appropriate on-task behaviour.
- *Private reprimand* – it is usually the case that a private reprimand is more effective than a public reprimand. A private reprimand is less likely to be received by the pupil as a put-down which the pupil may feel he or she has to respond to assertively and perhaps aggressively in order to impress fellow pupils. Private reprimands should consist of verbal disapproval of the inappropriate behaviour and a clear statement of the behaviour expected. The private reprimand can be delivered to the pupil in a quiet voice as the teacher stands close to the pupil inspecting his or her work. If the pupil wishes to debate the issue such discussion should be deferred until the end of the lesson or to some other convenient time so that the teacher has time to listen to and respond to the pupil and the pupil can engage in the dialogue without having to take into account 'listening peers'.
- *Public reprimand* – sometimes a pupil misbehaves inappropriately in a very public, challenging manner. In this case a public reprimand is appropriate both to curtail the inappropriate behaviour and to communicate to the rest of the class that such behaviour is inappropriate. If a substantial number of the pupils in a class are misbehaving then a clear assertive public reprimand to the class as a whole is indicated. When reprimanding an individual pupil the reprimand should be prefaced by the pupil's name so that other pupils do not mistakenly challenge the teacher because they feel the reprimand was unfairly directed at them. A reprimand should always include a clear description of the unacceptable behaviour and the alternative acceptable behaviour.
- *Time out* – if a pupil persistently fails to respond to warning cues and personalised reprimands then the teacher could face a dilemma. On the one hand, the rules of the classroom are being subverted and a coping response from the teacher is required to maintain the credibility of the rules; on the other hand, if the teacher persists in attempting to achieve pupil compliance a major classroom incident may develop, and, in addition, during the time the teacher is dealing with the situation the other pupils in the class are being deprived of teaching time. Because of these considerations a strategy of *deferred consequences* should be implemented, i.e. a response should be made that allows for the situation to be dealt with at a later time. Sometimes a statement to the pupil such as, 'John, we'll deal with this matter at the end of the lesson', will be successful in sustaining teacher authority with the disruptive pupil remaining in the classroom. On other occasions the disruptive pupil may persist in their behaviour and be sent out of the classroom (known as 'time out').

It is important that 'time out' should be planned within the context of a whole school policy of pupil management: it should not be used at the discretion of an individual teacher. When a pupil is sent out of the classroom

- the pupil should be sent to a *specific room* or area;
- the room or area should *be supervised* by a teacher;
- a system should be in place to *support the class teacher* in dealing with the pupil behaviour which necessitated time out.

If the arrangements described above are not in place then the pupil sent out of the classroom may 'hang around' outside the classroom door and intentionally or unintentionally distract the other pupils. Such pupil behaviour could or will attract further teacher attention, as well as teacher warnings or threats of dire negative consequences if the pupil does not desist. The likelihood of this further teacher warning or threat producing pupil compliance is low – for this strategy was unsuccessful when the pupil was still in the classroom situation. However the possibility exists that the pupil may carry on challenging the teacher by persisting in non-compliant challenging behaviour. This possibility has the consequence of distracting the teacher away from the task of teaching the rest of the pupils – and it could be that the other pupils start to misbehave. Another scenario is the possibility that the pupil will wander down the corridor distracting other classes of pupils and/or their teachers.

### Time out room or Personal Guidance Unit?

Tensions can exist when provision is made for pupils whose behaviour warrants exclusion from the classroom. Conflicting philosophies might exist over the purpose of placement in such a facility. Time out has at least two functions:

(i)     As a punishing consequence for inappropriate classroom behaviour. There are two aspects to the punishment: (a) removal from the classroom – which is assumed to be a reinforcing environment, if only because of the presence of the peer group; and (b) placement in the time out room – a room not designed either by decor or activities to be particularly reinforcing.

(ii)    As a result of the above, for the pupil to behave appropriately when reinstated in mainstream lessons.

In the light of these functions it is not an unreasonable assertion that time out, if used, should be of short duration.

However there may be pupils who do not respond positively to a time out procedure, i.e. behaviour change, if it occurs, is transitory. Other pupils may reject the attempt to change and control their behaviour. In either of the above cases prolonged placement in a time out facility would be inappropriate. These are two pragmatic grounds for not using time out. In addition some educationalists argue that if a pupil is not responding appropriately to the demands of the classroom then a 'helping response', not a 'punitive response' is called for.

The term Pupil Guidance Unit has 'helping' as opposed to 'punitive' connotations. Placement in such a facility would tend to be longer than in a time out facility. The reason for this is that often the pupil's chronic classroom misbehaviour is a consequence of either *lack of commitment* to the behavioural standards of the school or *social skill deficits*. In the former case the pupil *may not want* to conform to the behavioural requirements of the school and in the latter case the pupil *may be unable to* conform to the requirements. In either case extensive individual pupil support may be required before mainstream class reintegration proves viable. This support can take many forms including Motivational Interviewing and Social Skills Training.

## Evaluative statatements

The use of evaluative statements towards the end of the lesson is a simple, non-intrusive strategy of proven effectiveness in helping to promote the level of pupil on-task behaviour. An evaluative statement can be considered 'macro-feedback" about the academic work and/or social behaviour of a class of pupils over the course of a lesson. It therefore contrasts with the 'micro-feedback' about specific incidents of appropriate/inappropriate academic work or social behaviour that occur at specific times during the course of the lesson. The effects of evaluative statements on appropriate pupil behaviour is enhanced if the evaluative statements make reference to the rules of the classroom. For example, the level of on-task behaviour of a class of 27 first year pupils was increased by 12 per cent (from 77 to 89 per cent) in a Geography lesson (McNamara 1988a). The strategy was:

(i)   explicit rules of the classroom reviewed at the start of the lesson
(ii)  at the end of the lesson make evaluative statements with reference to the rules of the classroom.

This intervention strategy resulted in an increase of on-task behaviour of five minutes in a 45 minute lesson (from 35 to 40 minutes).

## SUMMARY

This chapter has described the place of classroom management techniques within a whole school approach to pupil management.

The success of any whole class or individual pupil management strategy is dependent upon a clear, accurate assessment of the problem behaviour – this can be achieved through the A-B-C analysis described ealier in this chapter. In parallel with this, appropriate pupil behaviours must be identified, communicated to the pupils and promoted.

Whilst acknowledging the multiple and diverse causes of pupil problem behaviour, the contents of this chapter focus on the most effective use of teacher time and skills, i.e. concentrating on classroom management practices.

The strategies outlined in this chapter are directed to:

(a) whole class interventions
(b) individual pupil interventions embedded in whole class interventions.

Whatever the 'level' of intervention chosen and, whatever the strategy used, both policies and practices have to be consistent, closely monitored and evaluated, in order to become *effective behaviour management tools.*

CHAPTER 3

# On-report: a positive approach

The aims of this chapter are to:

(i)    facilitate an evaluation of the present school practice of on-report;
(ii)   describe current theory of effective behaviour change;
(iii)  present a number of on-report protocols;
(iv)   illuminate the link between the theory of behaviour change and the practice of on-report;
(v)    facilitate a re-evaluation of the present school practice of on-report as a contribution to identifying improvements that can be made.

Pupil management programmes based on classroom management strategies, e.g. rules and positive teacher–pupil interactions, have a history of proven success. While such teacher practices are effective, a limitation is that the success is confined to the situation in which the programme is used, i.e. there is little evidence that change in pupil behaviour will occur in other classes. Consequently, if a pupil exhibits disruptive behaviour in three curriculum areas (e.g. RE, French, Geography) and a behaviour management programme is put into place in RE, it is likely that the management programme will be effective in the RE lesson but the pupil's behaviour in French and Geography will remain unchanged, i.e. generalisation of behaviour change is unlikely to occur.

The on-report system is a response to pupil misbehaviour that overcomes this problem of lack of generalisation, for the system is a 'portable response' which can be taken from lesson to lesson and can therefore be utilised across all curriculum areas – therefore lack of generalisation is not an issue.

## ON-REPORT: AN APPRAISAL OF CURRENT PRACTICE

Some schools have had a pupil management or 'discipline' policy for many years and since the publication of the Elton Report *Discipline in Schools* (1989), most schools have reached this position. Indeed most schools include an on-report system in the school's pupil management practices (McNamara 1985), but the effectiveness of on-report is often less than it might be (McNamara 1986).

A pupil management policy is a necessary but not sufficient condition for successful pupil management practices: for the practices, which are the vehicle for policy implementation, must be effective. A Checklist for a self-appraisal of the school's on-report system is presented in Figure 3.1. Completion of this Checklist provides the opportunity to assess current school on-report practices and the rationale underpinning them. After reading this chapter – which describes 'good practice' – a re-evaluation of current school practices can be undertaken. Furthermore, consideration can be given to ways of developing current practices.

| | YES / NO | NOT SURE |
|---|---|---|
| 1. Do you have an on-report system? | | |
| 2. What is the rationale for the on-report system? | *Describe on a separate sheet* | |
| 3. What is the purpose of the on-report system? | | |
| 4. Does the on-report system have a negative bias? | | |
| 5. Is the on-report system 'crafted' to ensure at least some positive recording? | | |
| 6. Are the target behaviours  i) specific? | | |
|     ii) observable? | | |
|     iii) positive? | | |
| 7. Is the on-report protocol reviewed with the pupil? | | |
| 8. Are parents involved in the monitoring of on-report? | | |

**Figure 3.1** On-report: an appraisal of current practice

## THE CODE OF PRACTICE

The *Code of Practice on the Identification and Assessment of Special Educational Needs* was published by the Department for Education in 1994. It places onerous responsibilities on schools: it could be said to constitute a kind of 'Highway Code' for the implementation of key parts of the Education Act 1993.

The Code of Practice describes a five stage model of assessment – and sole responsibility for assessment at Stages 1 and 2 rests with the school. The Government plans to amalgamate Stages 1 and 2 into a single 'school response' stage (DfEE 1998).

Stage 3 assessment may include assessment by Support Services external to the school. However the availability and therefore involvement of Support Services is variable across the country. This may be due to the contraction of Local Authority Support Services as budget pressures reduce the monies available. In addition, this contraction may have been added to by the delegation of monies to schools as part of the Local Management of Schools (LMS) legislation. The Government plans to to identify this stage as the 'school plus' stage.

In Local Education Authorities (LEAs) in which Support Service monies have been delegated to schools, responsibility for that part of the Stage 3 assessment previously carried out by the Support Service rests with the school: in LEAs in which Support Service availability is limited or not available, Stage 3 assessment responsibility also rests with the school.

Stage 2 and Stage 3 assessments involve devising an Individual Education Plan (IEP). The IEP incorporates one or more Individual Educational Programmes. Confusion may exist between an Individual Educational Plan and Individual Educational Programme. The differences between the two are described in the Appendix to this chapter. The Code of Practice recommends that the Individual Educational Plan is reviewed at least twice (Stage Review) before moving to Stage 4 Statutory Assessment.

As part of the Stage Review the pupil's response to each Individual Educational Programme is reviewed. This is a crucial exercise since the effectiveness of the Programme is evaluated. If the Stage 3 Programme has proved effective the pupil will remain at Stage 3 or perhaps move back to Stage 2: where the programme has proved less than effective then it may be that the school will request the LEA to agree to a Stage 4 Statutory Assessment.

When considering such a request for a Stage 4 Statutory Assessment the LEA will review evidence that the programmes of support at Stages 2 and 3 have been rigorously planned, implemented, monitored and evaluated. The use of appropriate on-report protocols can contribute to putting such a case to the LEA, for on-report protocols can:

(i)    objectively and explicitly help with the identification of problem behaviours; and,

(ii)   provide a focus to ensure that the Individual Educational Programme targets the problem behaviours.

The Stage Review is then focused on the success or otherwise of the intervention (Individual Educational Programme) – and the recording and reporting of the whole exercise constitutes a persuasive activity in the context of 'due process' when considering a move to a Stage 4 Statutory Assessment.

## ON-REPORT

### History and rationale

The on-report system had its origins in the early 1960s. In its original form the system took the form of a blank lesson timetable. The practice was for the pupil who was on-report to proffer the timetable to the teacher at the end of each lesson. The objective was for a 'satisfactory' rating to be given by the teacher, indicating that inappropriate behaviour had not occurred.

The pupil was placed on-report as a *punishment* and the intent was to suppress inappropriate behaviour, see Figure 3.2. Such a practice has withstood the test of time and therefore on pragmatic grounds alone has proved to be useful.

However there are shortcomings associated with the original practice of on-report: advances in the theory and practice of human behaviour change have yielded theoretical and practical indicators as to how the effectiveness of on-report practices can be increased.

Name......*James Has*.................................    Tutor Group ......*4S*...............    Date ....*21/1/96*.............

| | 1 | 2 | 3 | 4 | 5 | 6 | 7 |
|---|---|---|---|---|---|---|---|
| **MONDAY** | Satisfactory JH | Satisfactory PH | Satisfactory EP | OK SR | No problem MJ | Satisfactory PM | Poor EM |
| **TUESDAY** | Satisfactory PH | Satisfactory EP | Satisfactory SR | Satisfactory EM | No home/wk PM | Satisfactory EM | Cheeky! JH |
| **WEDNESDAY** | Late for lesson EP | Satisfactory SR | Satisfactory EM | Satisfactory JH | Satisfactory EM | Satisfactory JH | Satisfactory PH |
| **THURSDAY** | Satisfactory SR | Satisfactory EM | Satisfactory JH | Satisfactory PH | Satisfactory JH | Satisfactory PH | Satisfactory EP |
| **FRIDAY** | Satisfactory EM | Satisfactory JH | Satisfactory PH | Satisfactory EP | Satisfactory PH | Satisfactory EP | Satisfactory SR |

**Figure 3.2** An 'original' on report protocol

The major shortcoming of the traditional practice of on-report is that it is negative in emphasis – its aim is to suppress inappropriate pupil behaviour. A more positive approach is to promote appropriate pupil behaviour. Necessarily, if one is successful in promoting appropriate behaviour, then simultaneously one has been successful in suppressing inappropriate behaviour – without recourse to negative, sanction orientated practices. Three decades of development in the area of the theory and practice of human behaviour change has yielded a number of general principles which are associated with effective behaviour change. The three most important principles with relevance to the on-report system are:

*specific* task demand
*observable* task demand
*positive* task demand.

### Specificity of task demand

Originally the task demand 'don't misbehave' was the message of the on-report system. This general type of exhortation is not very efficient in bringing about behaviour change – although it is probably more effective than exhortations such as 'act your age', 'grow up'. The effectiveness of a task demand is enhanced by making it specific, i.e. by eliminating the possibilities of either:

– lack of agreement occurring between teacher and pupil as to what the task demand was, or
– whether the task demand was achieved.

This latter consideration generates a second principle for increasing the effectiveness of a task demand – namely that the task demand should be observable and therefore verifiable.

### Observable task demand

An effective task demand would be 'arrive at lessons on time' as this is specific, observable and verifiable. A less effective task demand would be 'try harder' or 'behave better' – for the constituent behaviours of trying harder and behaving better are not defined. Therefore the monitoring of task achievement by both the teacher and the pupil is a very subjective activity which can give rise to honest differences of opinion between the teacher and pupil. These differences can in turn give rise to conflict – whereas the intent of the exercise is to effect change in pupil behaviour and thereby reduce the probability of teacher–pupil conflict.

### Positive task demand

The negative emphasis of the on-report system can readily be eliminated and replaced by a positive emphasis without making any extra demands on teacher time; and, at the same time, increase the effectiveness of the on-report system as a strategy for effecting change in pupil behaviour. In addition, the function of the on-report system to record information about the occurrence of inappropriate behaviour is not lost.

Thus threefold improvements can be made to the on-report system:

(i)   change the emphasis from negative to positive
(ii)  increase the effectiveness as a behaviour change strategy
(iii) provide information about the occurrence of inappropriate behaviour.

These improvements are achieved by *monitoring the occurrence of appropriate behaviours*. For example, rather than recording when a pupil is late for a lesson, arrival on time is monitored; rather than recording when a pupil arrives at a lesson without equipment, arriving with equipment is monitored. The advantages and increased effectiveness of a positive on-report system occur because:

- *Pupil compliance* with the management programme is promoted because the emphasis is on recording desirable behaviours and this can be rewarding. In contrast it is not a pleasant activity to collect and record data about undesirable behaviours. The consequence of having to receive, accept and respond to data reflecting the occurrence of undesirable behaviour can be avoided by the pupil not cooperating with the on-report system, 'losing' the on-report card and so on.
- *Appropriate behaviour may be promoted* – the recognition and recording of appropriate behaviour may increase the frequency of occurrence of the behaviour: for teacher recognition and recording can function as a positive reinforcement, thereby increasing the frequency of occurrence of the behaviour(s) recorded.

- *There is no loss of information* involved in positive monitoring – the absence of a record of the appropriate behaviour indicates the occurrence of the corresponding inappropriate behaviour: if 'arrived on time' is not recorded then 'arrived late' is the message.

Some teachers are most comfortable when the on-report protocol facilitates the recording of both appropriate and inappropriate behaviours. Such a practice certainly facilitates an easy visual inspection and analysis of the data. Such an on-report protocol is reproduced in Figure 3.3.

## EXAMPLES OF ON-REPORT PROTOCOLS

### The Improved Behaviour Record

Comments on the Improved Behaviour Record shown in Figure 3.3.

(i)    This on-report protocol lists a range of desirable classroom behaviours and the corresponding undesirable behaviours. For both, two spaces are available for additional pupil specific behaviours to be added if required.

(ii)   The layout of the protocol is such that a target of achieving 'all ticks above the line' can be set.

(iii)  The protocol is shown to the teacher *at the beginning of the lesson*, stays on the pupil's desk *during the lesson*, and is completed by the teacher at the *end of the lesson*. Consequently:

   (a) the teacher is made aware at the beginning of the lesson that a particular pupil's behaviour has to be rated at the end of the lesson;

   (b) the pupil has a constant visual reminder on the desk that the teacher will assess his or her behaviour during the lesson and rate it at the end of the lesson: this visual reminder might also stimulate the pupil to self-monitor and self-evaluate his or her own behaviour during the course of the lesson, i.e. act as a reminder.

(iv)   Some teachers adopt the practice of keeping the on-report protocol on their desk during the lesson: when this is the case the benefits described in (b) above are lost.

(v)    In schools in which many lessons are 'double periods' it is recommended that the on-report protocol is completed by the teacher at the end of each period (i.e. twice in a double period lesson). This is recommended because the teacher assessment provides feedback to the pupil, and positive feedback in the form of positive teacher assessments can be reinforcing – thus increasing the likelihood of continued improved behaviour on the part of the pupil.

(vi)   The on-report system is a powerful strategy for facilitating change in pupil behaviour, but there will be occasions when the behaviour change does not occur or is transitory. In such situations the on-report system will not have fulfilled the function of a behaviour change facilitator: but the data collected using the on-report protocol will have contributed to the assessment and constitute a database for a further problem analysis and intervention.

# IMPROVED BEHAVIOUR RECORD

NAME .......... *Elvis Sweeny* .......... FORM ...... *3R* ...... DATE ...... *13/1/96* ......

Please

    i)    Show this form to the teacher at the BEGINNING of each lesson

    ii)   Keep this form on your desk DURING the lesson

    iii)  Ask the teacher to complete the form at the END of each lesson

                     Thank you

| | Lesson | | | | | | |
|---|---|---|---|---|---|---|---|
| | 1 | 2 | 3 | 4 | 5 | 6 | 7 |
| 1. Arrived on time for Lesson | ✓ | | ✓ | ✓ | ✓ | ✓ | ✓ |
| 2. Brought Equipment | ✓ | | ✓ | ✓ | ✓ | ✓ | ✓ |
| 3. Homework Done / Done well* on Time | ✓ | | | ✓ | ✓ | ✓ | ✓ |
| 4. Attentive During Lesson | ✓ | | | ✓ | ✓ | ✓ | ✓ |
| 5. Not Disturbing Others | ✓ | | | ✓ | ✓ | ✓ | ✓ |
| 6. Followed Instructions | ✓ | | | ✓ | ✓ | ✓ | ✓ |
| 7. Completed Classwork | ✓ | | | ✓ | ✓ | ✓ | ✓ |
| 8. School Award Given | ✓ | | | ✓ | ✓ | ✓ | ✓ |
| 9. Sensible Behaviour | ✓ | | | ✓ | ✓ | ✓ | ✓ |
| 10. Polite and Well Mannered | ✓ | | | ✓ | | ✓ | ✓ |
| 11. | | | | | | | |
| 12. | | | | | | | |

| | | | | | | | |
|---|---|---|---|---|---|---|---|
| 1. Late to Lesson | | ✓ | | | | | |
| 2. Inadequate / No Equipment* | | ✓ | | | | | |
| 3. Homework Not Done / Not Completed* on Time | | ✓ | ✓ | | | | |
| 4. Inattentive During Lesson | | ✓ | ✓ | | | | |
| 5. Disturbing Others | | ✓ | ✓ | | | | |
| 6. Not Following Instructions | | ✓ | ✓ | | | | |
| 7. Insufficient Classwork | | ✓ | ✓ | | | | |
| 8. Lines, Detention Not Completed | | ✓ | ✓ | | | | |
| 9. Silly Behaviour | | ✓ | ✓ | | | | |
| 10. Impolite and Ill-mannered | | ✓ | ✓ | | | | |
| 11. | | ✓ | ✓ | | | | |
| 12. | | | | | | | |
| Teacher's Initials | | | | | | | |

*  *Delete as applicable*

**Parental Signature** ...........................................................................

*(Required: yes/no)*

**Figure 3.3** The Improved Behaviour Record

(vii)  A strength of the on-report protocol reproduced in Figure 3.3 is the range of behaviours included. It is unlikely that a pupil will be negatively evaluated in all the areas assessed: therefore opportunities will be available to the monitoring teachers to focus on some positive pupil behaviours before addressing the problematic behaviours. Given something positive to build on by recognising the occurrence of some appropriate behaviours, the likelihood of the pupil remaining 'engaged' in the behaviour change programme is greater than if little or no success is recorded and no positive feedback is given.

(viii)  It may be validly argued that to rate the occurrence or non occurrence of ten or more behaviours when perhaps only one or two pupil behaviours are of concern is unnecessary and perhaps too time consuming. An example of a less extensive on-report protocol is illustrated in Figure 3.4.

The following comments relate to the Responsible Pupil Record (Figure 3.4).

(i)  The protocol presented in Figure 3.4 is designed to monitor a pupil's punctuality, personal organisation, social behaviour and academic work output. In addition the on-report protocol can be personalised by the addition of up to three other specific behaviours of concern. For example, 'Not disturbing other pupils' may be an identified behaviour to be encouraged: this could therefore be added to the list of behaviours to be monitored (see Figure 3.4).

(ii)  The 'Further Comments' column allows individual teachers to make specific comments about aspects of the pupil's classroom behaviour, record reinforcing comments and so on.

(iii)  Communication to home: pupils do perceive a letter home as a powerful consequence – as a reward if the contents are positive and contain 'good news' and as a punishment if the contents are negative and contain 'bad news'. The power of the communication home can be harnessed to the on-report system by sending the on-report protocol home each day. Some teachers use the on-report system for solely school based purposes in the first instance and extend it to include a parental dimension only if the pupil's initial response to being on-report is not satisfactory. The on-report protocol illustrated in Figure 3.4 includes the message-home dimension.

(iv)  The assessment system is twofold. For the behaviours 'Punctuality' and 'Equipment' a simple yes/no response is required. For 'Behaviour' and 'Work Output' a graded response from 1 (Very Poor) to 5 (Very Good) is invited. This latter range of possible responses (from 1 to 5) allows for differential feedback to be given to the pupil. Consequently small improvements in pupil behaviour can be reflected, 'captured' and fed back to the pupil. Thus if a pupil's rating moves from 1 (Very Poor) to 2 (Poor) this 'improvement' can be reflected in the feedback given to the pupil and thereby have the potential to shape up the pupil's behaviour so that the 'Poor' behaviour can in turn be shaped up to progress towards 'Satisfactory' and beyond. If assessment of behaviour had been restricted to 'Satisfactory/unsatisfactory' then a discrimination between the pupil's behaviour on the two occasions would not have been possible. Finer differentiation and feedback can be achieved by extending the scale from 5 to 10 points. Thus 2 might equal 'Very Poor', 4 'Poor', 6 'Satisfactory', 8 'Good' and 10 'Very Good': but finer judgements and feedback can be made/given by using the values 0, 1, 3, 5, 7 and 9.

**THE RESPONSIBLE PUPIL RECORD**

| | Pupil must fill in this column | Punctuality (*) | Equipment (*) | Behaviour (**) | Work Output (**) | Not disturbing other pupils (**) | | | FURTHER COMMENTS | Teacher's Signature |
|---|---|---|---|---|---|---|---|---|---|---|
| a.m. Registration | | / | | / | | | | | | |
| Lesson 1 | | | | | | | | | | |
| Lesson 2 | | | | | | | | | | |
| Lesson 3 | | | | | | | | | | |
| Lesson 4 | | | | | | | | | | |
| p.m. Registration | | / | | / | | | | | | |
| Lesson 5 | | | | | | | | | | |
| Lesson 6 | | | | | | | | | | |
| Lesson 7 | | | | | | | | | | |

NAME ..................................... DATE ....................

\* yes / no  \*\* 1 = Very Poor
2 = Poor
3 = Satisfactory
4 = Good
5 = Very Good

Parent or Guardian's Comment and Signature
(Required yes / no)                                    Signed ...............................................

**Figure 3.4** The Responsible Pupil Record

(v)   The above considerations should not be interpreted as indicating that 'satisfactory/unsatisfactory' ratings of pupil behaviour should never be used: they are presented so that informed decisions can be made about the most appropriate form the on-report protocol should take for a particular pupil in a particular situation.

(vi)  The quantification of assessment facilitated by the rating system for academic work output and behaviour involved in this on-report protocol creates the opportunity for the practice of goal setting to be incorporated into the on-report programme. An example of such an on-report protocol is presented in Figure 3.5.

## The Behavioural Achievement Record

Comments relating to the Behavioural Achievement Record (Figure 3.5) are as follows.

(i)   This on-report protocol simply lists two general aspects to be assessed, i.e. 'Behaviour' and 'Work'. They are rated on a scale 1 to 5. It may be that the specific constituent behaviours that make up appropriate 'behaviour' and appropriate 'work' are understood by the pupil or are made known to the pupil at the time of going on-report. The most important feature of this on-report protocol is that it has the potential to

**BEHAVIOUR ACHIEVEMENT RECORD**

NAME...... *Charles Edwards* ...... FORM...... *3C* ...... DATE ...... *6/6/94* ......

...... *Charles* ......is on-report: to help ...... *Charles* ...... with his / her work and behaviour in the classroom.

When ...... *Charles* ......has received...... *700* ......marks...... *Charles* ......will attempt to continue

working and behaving in an acceptable manner without the help of the on-report system.

| | LESSON | | | | | | | Total | Parent's Signature | | RATING SCALE | |
|---|---|---|---|---|---|---|---|---|---|---|---|---|
| | 1 | 2 | 3 | 4 | 5 | 6 | 7 | | | | 1 | Very Poor |
| Monday | • CF | • EB | • KH | • DW | • JM | • CS | • RD | | | | 2 | Poor |
| | 1 2 3 4 5 | 1 2 3 4 5 | 1 2 3 4 5 | 1 2 3 4 5 | 1 2 3 4 5 | 1 2 3 4 5 | 1 2 3 4 5 | | | | 3 | Class Average |
| Behaviour | ✓ | ✓ | ✓ | ✓ | ✓ | | ✓ | 26 | PE | | 4 | Good |
| Work | ✓ | ✓ | ✓ | ✓ | ✓ | | ✓ | 23 | | | 5 | Very Good |
| Tuesday | 1 2 3 4 5 | 1 2 3 4 5 | 1 2 3 4 5 | 1 2 3 4 5 | 1 2 3 4 5 | 1 2 3 4 5 | 1 2 3 4 5 | | | • Teacher's Signature | | |
| Behaviour | | | | | | | | | | | | |
| Work | | | | | | | | | | | | |
| Wednesday | 1 2 3 4 5 | 1 2 3 4 5 | 1 2 3 4 5 | 1 2 3 4 5 | 1 2 3 4 5 | 1 2 3 4 5 | 1 2 3 4 5 | | | | | |
| Behaviour | | | | | | | | | | | | |
| Work | | | | | | | | | | | | |
| Thursday | 1 2 3 4 5 | 1 2 3 4 5 | 1 2 3 4 5 | 1 2 3 4 5 | 1 2 3 4 5 | 1 2 3 4 5 | 1 2 3 4 5 | | | | | |
| Behaviour | | | | | | | | | | | | |
| Work | | | | | | | | | | | | |
| Friday | 1 2 3 4 5 | 1 2 3 4 5 | 1 2 3 4 5 | 1 2 3 4 5 | 1 2 3 4 5 | 1 2 3 4 5 | 1 2 3 4 5 | | | | | |
| Behaviour | | | | | | | | | | | | |
| Work | | | | | | | | | | | | |

Remember loss of Achievement Record results in the loss of all marks.

Please:-

(✓ or X)

| | M | T | W | T | F |
|---|---|---|---|---|---|
| i) Show the Achievement Record to the teacher at the beginning of each lesson........................... | ✓ | | | | |
| ii) Keep the Achievement Record on the desk during the lesson........................................ | ✓ | | | | |
| iii) Ask the teacher to rate your work and behaviour at the end of each lesson........................... | ✓ | | | | |
| iv) Take the Achievement Record home each evening for your parents to discuss with you and sign. | ✓ | | | | |
| v) Report to ...... *H. O'Year* ...... each morning with your Record. ................................ | ✓ | | | | |

**GOOD LUCK !**

**Figure 3.5** The Behaviour Achievement Record

- harness the motivational effects of *setting goals*
- benefit from the reinforcing consequence of *goal achievement.*

(ii) The rating of 'Behaviour' and 'Work' for each lesson provides the opportunity to set *short, medium* and *long term goals*

- up to 10 points can be gained per lesson (short term goal)
- up to 70 points can be gained in a day (medium term goal)
- up to 350 points can be gained in a week (long term goal).

(iii) This on-report protocol contrasts markedly with that illustrated in Figure 3.3: for whereas the protocol illustrated in Figure 3.5 invites a rating of the pupil's performance in two general areas, academic work and social behaviour, the Figure 3.3 protocol invites a dichotomous satisfactory/unsatisfactory rating of a range of specific behaviours. Thus the former rating system allows for *discriminative feedback* to be given to the pupil whereas the dichotomous rating does not. However there are some specific problem areas for which dichotomous ratings are very appropriate (see Figure 3.6).

**THE 'BE PREPARED' RECORD**

| | | | MON | TUES | WED | THURS | FRI | | Signature |
|---|---|---|---|---|---|---|---|---|---|
| NAME *Audrey Swan* FORM *4S* DATE *18/1/96* | | | | | | | | | |

Subject Teacher: please mark the box as appropriate:

✓  =  satisfactory
x  =  unsatisfactory
n/a  =  not applicable

| LESSON | SUBJECT | | MON | TUES | WED | THURS | FRI | | Signature |
|---|---|---|---|---|---|---|---|---|---|
| 1 | M *FRENCH* T W T F | BOOK(S) | ✓ | | | | | M | *MJ* |
| | | EQUIPMENT | ✓ | | | | | T W | |
| | | PUNCTUAL | ✓ | | | | | T | |
| | | HOMEWORK | ✓ | | | | | F | |
| 2 | M *GEOG.* T W T F | BOOK(S) | ✓ | | | | | M | *JM* |
| | | EQUIPMENT | ✓ | | | | | T W | |
| | | PUNCTUAL | ✓ | | | | | T | |
| | | HOMEWORK | ✓ | | | | | F | |
| 3 | M *CDT* T W T F | BOOK(S) | ✓ | | | | | M | *PS* |
| | | EQUIPMENT | ✓ | | | | | T W | |
| | | PUNCTUAL | ✓ | | | | | T | |
| | | HOMEWORK | n/a | | | | | F | |
| 4 | M *HISTORY* T W T F | BOOK(S) | ✓ | | | | | M | *JT* |
| | | EQUIPMENT | ✓ | | | | | T W | |
| | | PUNCTUAL | ✓ | | | | | T | |
| | | HOMEWORK | ✓ | | | | | F | |
| 5 | M *ENGLISH* T W T F | BOOK(S) | ✓ | | | | | M | *JH* |
| | | EQUIPMENT | ✓ | | | | | T W | |
| | | PUNCTUAL | ✓ | | | | | T | |
| | | HOMEWORK | X | | | | | F | |
| 6 | M *BIOLOGY* T W T F | BOOK(S) | ✓ | | | | | M | *MJ* |
| | | EQUIPMENT | ✓ | | | | | T W | |
| | | PUNCTUAL | ✓ | | | | | T | |
| | | HOMEWORK | n/a | | | | | F | |
| 7 | M *RE* T W T F | BOOK(S) | ✓ | | | | | M | *SC* |
| | | EQUIPMENT | ✓ | | | | | T W | |
| | | PUNCTUAL | ✓ | | | | | T | |
| | | HOMEWORK | n/a | | | | | F | |

**Figure 3.6** The 'Be Prepared' Record

## The 'Be Prepared' Record

The 'Be Prepared' protocol (Figure 3.6) allows an 'assessment at a glance' to be made of a pupil's state of preparation for lessons over a period of a week. The intention is that the pupil will be prepared because of the monitoring, but, as with all intervention programmes, there is an assessment function, i.e. the pupil's response to intervention.

Personal organisation difficulties are associated with other difficulties as well as existing in their own right as in cases of dyslexia, dyspraxia and other specific learning difficulties.

Sometimes a specific pupil behaviour or class of behaviours is the sole cause for concern – arriving late to lessons, arriving without PE kit, not completing homework. In such situations it may be appropriate to focus just on the problem behaviour. This can be done by utilising a one behaviour or one class of behaviours on-report protocol such as that illustrated in Figure 3.7

**LESSON ATTENDANCE RECORD**

WEEK COMMENCING.............*27/6/94*.................

Please initial if ...............*Brian Smith*...............attended your lesson.

Thank you

| | SESSION / LESSON | | | | | | | | | Parent's Signature |
|---|---|---|---|---|---|---|---|---|---|---|
| | Reg | 1 | 2 | Brk | 3 | 4 | Lun | 5 | 6 | 7 | |
| MONDAY | | AS | RT | | SM | NP | | MC | JB | LC | *S. Smith* |
| TUESDAY | | BP | LL | | KW | JB | | LR | NP | PB | *S. Smith* |
| WEDNESDAY | | | | | | | | | | | |
| THURSDAY | | | | | | | | | | | |
| FRIDAY | | | | | | | | | | | |

**Figure 3.7** Lesson Attendance Record

## The Lesson Attendance Record

Internal truancy – a pupil registering as attending school but subsequently not attending some or even all of his or her lessons – is not an uncommon problem. A specific on-report protocol to address this problem is presented in Figure 3.7.

## The Behaviour Target Record

Figure 3.8 demonstrates a first example of a Behaviour Target Record. This is similar to the Behaviour Achievement Record illustrated in Figure 3.5. However

**BEHAVIOUR TARGET RECORD**

NAME.......*John Small*....... FORM.......*3S*....... DATE .......*2/1/96*.......

.......*John*.......is trying to improve his / her behaviour in the classroom and around the school.

.......*John*.......has agreed to avoid engaging in the behaviours listed below.

.......*John's*.......behaviour will be rated according to the following scale:–

1 = No cause for concern    2 = Mild cause for concern    3 = Serious cause for concern

Thank you

| BEHAVIOURS | SESSION / LESSON | | | | | | | | | |
|---|---|---|---|---|---|---|---|---|---|---|
| | Reg | 1 | 2 | Brk | 3 | 4 | Lun | 5 | 6 | 7 |
| 1. *Shouts out in lessons* | | 1 | 1 | | 1 | 1 | | 1 | 1 | 1 |
| 2. *Packs away early* | | 1 | 1 | | 1 | 1 | | 1 | 1 | 1 |
| 3. *Threatens other pupils* | | 1 | 1 | | 1 | 1 | | 2 | 2 | 3 |
| Teachers initials | | MJ | EM | | JB | NP | | SM | MB | VC |

Parent's Signature .......*S. Smith*.......
(Required yes / no)

**Figure 3.8** Behaviour Target Record (example 1)

the Behaviour Target Record focuses on particular pupil behaviours of concern, that is, it adheres to the principle of specificity of task demand. The theme of this book is positive pupil management. However there is a place for focusing on inappropriate pupil behaviour(s) provided that this focus is embedded in a pupil management programme which has an overall positive emphasis.

The second example of the Behaviour Target Record, illustrated in Figure 3.9, includes the practice of deducting points if specific undesirable behaviours occur. Thus George (see Figure 3.9) caused disruption by shouting out in lessons, threatening other pupils and packing away early: therefore a particular negative consequence (the loss of one point) was made contingent upon each occurrence of any one of these behaviours.

**BEHAVIOUR TARGET RECORD**

NAME *George Black*  FORM *4B*  DATE *12/2/94*

*George* is trying to improve his / her behaviour in the classroom and around the school.

*George* has agreed to avoid engaging in the behaviours listed below:-

*George* has been credited with 3 points per lesson (one per behaviour).

Please deduct one point each time *George* engages in any of the behaviours listed.

Insert the number of points remaining in the appropriate cell.

Each week *George* retains *90* points he / she will be awarded a 'Certificate of Effort'

and a letter will be sent to his / her parents containing the 'good news'.

| BEHAVIOURS | SESSION / LESSON | | | | | | | | | |
|---|---|---|---|---|---|---|---|---|---|---|
| | Reg | 1 | 2 | Brk | 3 | 4 | Lun | 5 | 6 | 7 |
| 1. *Shouts out in lessons* | | 0 | 1 | | 1 | 1 | | 1 | 1 | 1 |
| 2. *Packs away early* | | 1 | 1 | | 1 | 1 | | 1 | 1 | 0 |
| 3. *Threatens other pupils* | | 1 | 1 | | 1 | 0 | | 1 | 1 | 1 |
| TOTAL | | 2 | 3 | | 3 | 2 | | 3 | 3 | 2 |
| Teachers initials | | *JS* | *BA* | | *AB* | *CE* | | *FR* | *SR* | *JS* |

| DAILY TOTAL | 18 |
|---|---|

*T. Black*
Parent's Signature ...................................................
(Required  yes / no)

**Figure 3.9** Behaviour Target Record (example 2)

## PREVENTIVE APPROACHES

The on-report response to pupil problem behaviour is reactive in that first the pupil misbehaves and then the teacher responds. However the creation of a positive pupil management environment within the school helps to further promote the occurrence of appropriate pupil behaviour and thus diminish the occurrence of inappropriate pupil behaviour, with a consequent reduction in the need to implement the practice of on-report.

Positive proactive pupil management practices consistent with those described earlier can be incorporated into a 'preventive' approach so that the appropriate behaviour of *all pupils* can be recognised, encouraged and promoted. For example, one school known to the author included in the school development plan the objective of achieving an explicit positive school ethos. Of particular relevance to this chapter is the method used to promote six specific pupil behaviours which were:

politeness
punctuality
journal management
personal organisation
responsible attitude
uniform compliance.

Some of these required pupil behaviours are less than specific, e.g. 'responsible attitude' and will no doubt be reviewed, but guidance is given to the teachers as illustrated in Table 3.1.

**Table 3.1** Pastoral Merit System criteria

| Behaviour | Evidence |
|---|---|
| 1. Politeness | 1. Polite conversation with staff ('please', 'thank you', 'Miss', 'Sir'). <br> 2. Polite conversation with other pupils. <br> 3. Not interrupting the teacher. <br> 4. Not jumping up at the end of the lesson. |
| 2. Organisation | 1. Homework complete. <br> 2. Homework handed in on time. <br> 3. Journal brought to school. <br> 4. Possess correct equipment/books. |
| 3. Uniform | 1. Correct uniform worn. <br> 2. Smart/tidy appearance. <br> 3. No graffiti on books/bags. |
| 4. Responsible Attitude | 1. Appropriate behaviour. <br> 2. Take care of equipment. <br> 3. Tidy up at end of lesson. |
| 5. Journal | 1. Record homework. <br> 2. Record date homework due. <br> 3. Obtain parent's signature. |
| 6. Punctuality | 1. Arrive at school on time. <br> 2. Arrive at lessons on time. |

**PASTORAL MERIT SYSTEM**

| MERITS | Lesson 1 | | | | | | Lesson 2 | | | | | | Lesson 3 | | | | | | Lesson 4 | | | | | | Lesson 5 | | | | | | Lesson 6 | | | | | | Lesson 7 | | | | | |
|---|---|---|---|---|---|---|---|---|---|---|---|---|---|---|---|---|---|---|---|---|---|---|---|---|---|---|---|---|---|---|---|---|---|---|---|---|---|---|---|---|---|---|
| | Teacher | | | | | | Teacher | | | | | | Teacher | | | | | | Teacher | | | | | | Teacher | | | | | | Teacher | | | | | | Teacher | | | | | |
| Day ............... Date ............... | Politeness | Organisation | Uniform | Responsible | Journal | Punctuality | Politeness | Organisation | Uniform | Responsible | Journal | Punctuality | Politeness | Organisation | Uniform | Responsible | Journal | Punctuality | Politeness | Organisation | Uniform | Responsible | Journal | Punctuality | Politeness | Organisation | Uniform | Responsible | Journal | Punctuality | Politeness | Organisation | Uniform | Responsible | Journal | Punctuality | Politeness | Organisation | Uniform | Responsible | Journal | Punctuality |

**Figure 3.10** The Daily Lesson Sheet

The method of encouraging these pupil behaviours is that a Daily Lesson Sheet is prepared for each form, who stay together during the school day as a teaching group. The Sheet consists of a list of form members. Across the top of the sheet are recorded the six behaviours listed above (see Figure 3.10).

As it would be too time consuming for each teacher to rate each pupil each lesson, no mark is placed in the appropriate 'box' if the pupil is credited with the behaviour. A mark (x) is made if the pupil's behaviour falls short of that required. After five weeks each pupil receives a 'credit' (stamped into the pupil's school journal) for each category of behaviour if no adverse mark has been received for the behaviour. When five credits are accumulated a merit certificate is presented to the pupil in assembly.

**Out of class behaviours**

In order to use an on-report approach to pupil management it is necessary for pupil behaviour to be observed and recorded/rated by an adult, usually a teacher, who is in a position of authority with respect to the pupil. In out of classroom situations the adult person may well be a non teacher, e.g. a dinner welfare assistant. On-report practices can be equally effective in out of classroom situations provided:

- the non teaching adult has the support and guidance of a teacher;
- the non teaching adult has received guidance about pupil management and the rationale underlying the practice of on-report;

– specific appropriate and inappropriate pupil behaviours relevant to the particular out of class situation are identified and made known to the non teaching adult and pupils.

When the above provisos are met, on-report protocols can be constructed to promote appropriate pupil behaviour.

### Out of school behaviours

Pupils sometimes misbehave off the school premises and therefore it is difficult, perhaps impossible, for a teacher or welfare assistant to monitor the pupils' behaviour. It is not uncommon for pupil behaviour on public transport (or specific school transport) to be a cause for concern. In such a situation pupil behaviour can be monitored by a responsible pupil – perhaps a school prefect if such are appointed. An example of such a report system is reproduced in Figure 3.11.

If such a practice is adopted the prefect will require support and training. The support can be provided by appointing a team of prefects. At a minimum the training should emphasise that the prefect's duty is to fulfill a reporting role, it is not to impose order on unruly pupils.

| Behaviour on School Transport Week Commencing:- | | Prefect's Sign. |
|---|---|---|
| **MONDAY** | **Pupil's behaviour was acceptable** | |
| Signatures Head of Year<br><br>Parent's | Pupil's behaviour was not acceptable — details | |
| **TUESDAY** | **Pupil's behaviour was acceptable** | |
| Signatures Head of Year<br><br>Parent's | Pupil's behaviour was not acceptable — details | |
| **WEDNESDAY** | **Pupil's behaviour was acceptable** | |
| Signatures Head of Year<br><br>Parent's | Pupil's behaviour was not acceptable — details | |
| **THURSDAY** | **Pupil's behaviour was acceptable** | |
| Signatures Head of Year<br><br>Parent's | Pupil's behaviour was not acceptable — details | |
| **FRIDAY** | **Pupil's behaviour was acceptable** | |
| Signatures Head of Year<br><br>Parent's | Pupil's behaviour was not acceptable — details | |
| **COMMENTS** | | |

**Figure 3.11** School Transport Report

## REVIEWING SKILLS

The process of positive restructuring is an essential feature of the reviewing process.

### *Positive restructuring*

Negative feedback can be unpleasant to pupils: the pupil can avoid this unpleasant consequence by opting out of the behaviour change programme, i.e. by not cooperating. Therefore to keep the pupil engaged in the programme, all feedback should be couched in positive terms whenever possible; for example:

- four late arrivals would be restructured 'You were early six times last week'
- being sent out of one lesson for misbehaviour would be restructured 'You completed 34 lessons last week'
- falling short of the lesson target in three lessons might be restructured in a number of ways: 'You achieved your lesson target 32 times last week'; 'You achieved your lesson target in every lesson on four days last week'; or 'You achieved your lesson target every morning last week and on two afternoons'.

Creativity has to be exercised to process the data so that the feedback of the data is couched positively.

The purpose of positive restructuring is to:

- emphasise and reinforce positive achievements
- facilitate consolidation of improvements in behaviour by recognising and reinforcing behaviour change
- facilitate explicit and realistic target setting by the pupil in the next phase of the programme.

Sometimes it may be helpful to include a non-problematic behaviour amongst the target behaviours. Such a practice ensures that there can be a positive focus at the start of the reviewing process, which can then 'lead to' review of the areas of behaviour of true concern.

The reviewing skills involve the teacher in helping the pupil to arrive at an action plan by encouraging the pupil to:

- review the current situation (and engage in positive restructuring)
- decide goals
- set targets
- plan strategies for target achievement.

The similarities between this approach to on-report practices (to promote appropriate behaviour) and accepted approaches to curriculum orientated action plans are readily apparent. This is helpful in that a consistent rationale can be brought to bear to the tasks of promoting appropriate pupil social and academic behaviour.

## A REAPPRAISAL OF CURRENT PRACTICE

Completion of the Checklist presented at the beginning of this chapter (Figure 3.1) facilitates an appraisal of the current school practices that constitute the on-report system and the thinking behind it. The questions that make up the

Checklist are derived from consideration of good practices – practices which have been described and justified in this chapter. The justification is derived from a consideration of the theory and practice of human behaviour change and from the implications of this for the practice of on-report.

To conclude this chapter you are invited to engage in three tasks:

(i)　Return to Figure 3.1 and examine your responses.

(ii)　Consider your responses in the light of the information presented in this chapter.

(ii)　Formulate a list of implications and actions to improve your current on-report system – or to devise one.

The third task can be facilitated by completing the Checklist presented in Figure 3.12. The fifth and perhaps the most important of the five aims of this chapter should now be achieved, namely:

to facilitate a reappraisal of the present school practice of on-report as a contribution to identifying improvements that can be made.

|  | Yes/No | Implications | Actions |
|---|---|---|---|
| 1. Do you have an on-report system? |  |  |  |
| 2. What is the rationale for the on-report system? | *Describe on a separate sheet* |  |  |
| 3. What is the purpose of the on-report system? |  |  |  |
| 4. Does the on-report system have a negative bias? |  |  |  |
| 5. Is the on-report system 'crafted' to ensure at least some positive recording? |  |  |  |
| 6. Are the target behaviours　　　i)　specific? |  |  |  |
| 　　　　　　　　　　　　　　　　　ii)　observable? |  |  |  |
| 　　　　　　　　　　　　　　　　　iii)　positive? |  |  |  |
| 7.　Is the on-report protocol reviewed with the pupil? |  |  |  |
| 8.　Are parents involved in the monitoring of on-report? |  |  |  |

**Figure 3.12** On-report: a reappraisal of current practice

## CONCLUDING OBSERVATIONS

A rationale for the on-report system has been presented, together with a number of examples of different on-report protocols. An understanding of the rationale has the potential to increase the effectiveness of the on-report system – for the supervising teacher is more able to respond flexibly both to the range of possible pupil problem behaviours and also to variations in pupil response to the on-report system. Ideally a teacher will have a bank of different on-report protocols from which to choose – as well as having a sufficient appreciation of the theory and practice of 'on-report' to 'tailor' the on-report protocol to the particular pupil and the particular presenting problem(s). In addition, an appreciation of the theory underlying the practice of on-report empowers the supervising teacher to 'trouble shoot' on-report protocols that do not elicit the desired change in pupil behaviour.

A good quality on-report protocol helps to convey to the pupil the message that the school and pupil together are engaged in a serious and important endeavour. However, a cautionary note: 'They're only bits of paper!' is a cynical response to the use of on-report protocols. Yes, they are: on-report protocols per se are unlikely to influence pupil behaviour: but the on-report protocol provides a focus and 'vehicle' for the teacher to work with the pupil to effect change in pupil behaviour. The skills required of the teacher are the same as the reviewing skills necessary when engaged in active pupil learning with the objective of identifying Individual Action Plans.

## APPENDIX

### *Terminology*

The abbreviation IEP can be a source of confusion: for IEP can stand for either an Individual Educational Programme or an Individual Educational Plan. Clarification of the two terms is best achieved in question and answer format as follows.

*What is an IEP?*
In terms of the Code of Practice an IEP is an Individual Plan.

*I thought an IEP was an Individual Education Programme?*
Yes, some Authorities use the term IEP to refer to an Individual Education Programme: pre the 1993 Education Act and the consequent Code of Practice most teachers and psychologists would have equated IEP with Individual Education Programme.

*What is the difference between IEP (plan) and an IEP (programme)?*
There are a number of differences both conceptual and practical: for example, the Plan is more wide ranging than the Programme – in fact, an IEP (programme) can be subsumed under the IEP (plan).

*Can you be more specific about what is involved in an Individual Education Plan?*
Yes, this is described in paragraph 2:93 of the Code of Practice. The Individual Educational Plan should set out:

1. Nature of the child's (learning) difficulties.
2. Action – special educational provision
   (a) staff involved, including frequency of support
   (b) specific programmes, activities, materials, equipment.
3. Help from parents at home.

4. Targets to be achieved in a given time.
5. Any pastoral care or medical requirements.
6. Monitoring and assessments arrangements.
7. Review arrangements and date.

*Can you identify in the above seven points the overlap of the Individual Educational Plan and the Individual Educational Programme?*
Yes, the Individual Educational Programme involves specific observable, measurable goals being described and targets leading to the goal(s) being made clear – but an Individual Educational Plan describes:

1. The specific programmes of work to be followed.
2. The materials/equipment required.
3. Activities/teaching methods.
4. Staff responsible for delivering the programme.
5. Staff time involved, i.e. frequency and length of teaching directed to delivering the programmes.
6. Parent involvement in delivering/consolidating the programmes (if involved).
7. Monitoring/assessment/review arrangements and date.

*It seems to be that there is a considerable overlap between the requirements of the Individual Educational Plan and the Individual Education Programme?*
Yes, there is. That is why it is crucial when talking about IEPs to make it perfectly clear whether one is referring to a Plan or a Programme.

*Can you summarise the difference between the Individual Educational Plan and the Individual Education Programme?*
A plan is an overall description of the child's current educational situation – difficulties, needs, means/methods of addressing the needs and the monitoring/reviewing arrangements in place to evaluate the effectiveness of the Plan. In contrast, a Programme focuses on specific areas of difficulty, identifies 'remedial' programmes to address the difficulties and assesses the effectiveness of the specific programme to address the specific problem. In other words it is possible that there could be a number of different Individual Educational Programmes subsumed within the overall Educational Plan.

# CHAPTER 4

# Behavioural contracts

The purposes of this chapter are to:

Describe the history, the theory, and the structure of behaviour contracts.
Present examples of behaviour contracts targeting problematic pupil behaviour(s).
Present examples of pupil–school contracts.
Present an example of a home–school contract.
Present a contract of 'last resort'.

## INTRODUCTION

Contracts form the basis of our social order. The use of contracts is normal in legal and business practice. Such contracts are usually written agreements stating the general expectation of each party and may specify bonuses for fulfilment and penalties for non-fulfilment of the contract. In contrast 'social contracts' are usually implicit and not recorded, i.e. the specific consequences of fulfilment and non-fulfilment are not spelt out. For example, if two people arrange to meet then this constitutes a social contract. However, specific consequences for breaking the contract are not usually spelt out in advance. If one person doesn't bother to turn up then the 'contract' is broken and social consequences will come into play – the injured party may not make arrangements to socialise with the unreliable person again. Written social contracts can be used to effect change in pupil behaviour. The use of written social contracts for this purpose can be considered an 'artificial' procedure in that it is not a normal social practice.

The overall aim is to withdraw the written contract while ensuring that the rules of the contract become rules for everyday conduct, i.e. the formal, written, explicit contract becomes a social, unwritten, implicit contract – which nonetheless contains the rules to generate good behaviour. Because written contracts usually focus on changing pupil behaviour they are often referred to as behavioural contracts.

## BEHAVIOURAL CONTRACTS

The aim of behavioural contracts is to schedule the exchange of positive reinforcement between the parties to the agreement, i.e. to structure people to 'be nice' to each other and to behave towards the other party as the other party would wish.

### Rationale

The effectiveness of any intervention strategy is enhanced if the rationale generating the strategy is explicit and understood: A knowledge of the 'developmental history' of behavioural contracting illuminates the applicability of the practice in educational settings.

Behavioural contracts had their origins in the work of Stuart (1971), and were first used in the context of family therapy involving delinquents. The focus of this book is management strategies for use in educational settings, but as the principles underlying behavioural contracts can be applied in educational settings so too can the practice of contracting.

Observational studies in the homes of delinquents revealed that the families of delinquents could be differentiated from the families of non-delinquents on two criteria:

(i)    Non-delinquent families were characterised by relatively high rates of positive reciprocal interactons and delinquent families by relatively low rates of positive reciprocal interactions (Stuart 1969), i.e. non-delinquent family interactions were characterised by the family members 'being nice' to each other.

(ii)   Delinquent families were characterised by higher rates of negative coercive interactions and non-delinquent families by lower rates of negative coercive interactions (Patterson and Reid 1971) – delinquent family interactions were characterised by the family members being threatening and intimidatory towards each other in order to 'get their own way'; in other words, 'not being nice to each other'.

It was these observational data from naturalistic studies of family interactions that influenced Stuart to tackle the problem of family disharmony by restructuring the family interactions – by promoting positive interactions and reducing negative interactions – and the vehicle he used to effect this restructuring was behavioural contracting.

Stuart put forward behavioural contracting as an effective means of promoting mutually reinforcing behaviour in family interactions. He based the practice on a number of assumptions, the more important of these being:

(a) Receipt of positive reinforcement (having people behave towards you as you would wish) is a privilege rather than a right.

(b) Effective interpersonal agreements are governed by the norm of reciprocity: each party has responsibilities/duties, as well as privileges.

(c) The value of an interpersonal exchange is related to the amount of positive reinforcement received in the exchange.

(d) Rules create freedom in interpersonal exchanges – as freedom depends upon the opportunity to make behavioural choices with the knowledge of the probable outcome of each alternative.

### The structure of behavioural contracts

The three essential elements of behavioural contracts are:

- *privileges:* a contract should detail the privileges each party can expect after first fulfilling certain responsibilities;
- *responsibilities:* a contract should detail the kinds of responsibilities essential to securing these privileges;
- *monitoring:* a contract should include some type of monitoring system to record contract compliance.

In addition to these essential elements of behavioural contracts there are two further desirable elements: bonuses and sanctions.

### The inclusion of a bonus

It is easier to achieve behaviour change in the short term than to sustain behaviour change over a longer period of time: compare success in giving up smoking for a few days (achieved by many smokers), with the more limited success achieved by smokers in giving up smoking for much longer periods of time or even permanently. Therefore, in addition to reinforcing specific contract compliance, it is desirable to reinforce extended periods of contract compliance. Thus a pupil may be reinforced for one day of non-disruptive behaviour – an admirable though perhaps unspectacular achievement for the pupil. However, five days of non-disruptive behaviour may be remarkable for the pupil – and this extended period of positive responding should be reinforced in its own right.

### The inclusion of sanctions

The inclusion of sanctions in a behavioural contract is perhaps surprising in the light of the positive emphasis of pupil management put forward in this book. It could be argued that non-receipt of privileges should be sufficient to punish non-compliance to contract responsibilities. However the inclusion of sanctions can be justified on the grounds that in certain circumstances the non-delivery of reinforcement (receipt of privileges) may be insufficient to stop an undesirable behaviour occuring. If a pupil is inclined to disrupt a lesson, the non-receipt of a 'satisfactory behaviour' rating may be an insufficient consequence to suppress the undesirable behaviour: but the additional sanction of 'loss of 25p pocket money' may just 'tip the balance' and stop the pupil's inappropriate behaviour.

Two further requirements characterise 'good' contracts: they are (a) a starting date; and (b) a renegotiation date.

### Why sign behavioural contracts?

Putting one's name to an agreement is an action not to be undertaken lightly in our society. Signed legal contracts can be enforced by law. The 'contracts' or 'agreements' entered into by pupils, parents and teachers are not enforceable by law; nonetheless, by signing the contract the signatories are making a statement to the effect that 'in signing the agreement I will be bound by the undertakings therein'. There is experimental evidence to support the assertion that there is a positive relationship between overt commitment and task compliance (Levy 1977).

Levy reported that when patients made a verbal commitment to follow a course of treatment, significantly more followed the course than did patients from an equivalent group that did not make a verbal commitment. However, when patients signed an agreement to follow a course of treatment, significantly more followed the course than did patients from the equivalent group that gave only a verbal commitment. Subsequent research reveals that the relationship between overt commitment and task compliance is more complex than Levy's initial study would indicate. Nonetheless the probability of agreement compliance is increased when the agreement is signed without coercion.

## BEHAVIOURAL CONTRACTS IN EDUCATIONAL SETTINGS

Many classroom observational studies of teacher–pupil interactions in classes of difficult to manage pupils yield data which parallels the data reported from studies of parent–delinquent children interactions. In particular there is an overemphasis on negative control on the part of teachers and as a consequence a lack of reciprocity (positive exchanges) between teacher and pupils.

In the school situation the justification for reciprocity referred to above can be derived from the following two educational propositions.

(i)   Pupils should be educated according to age, aptitude and ability and treated with dignity, fairness and respect (the pupils' privilege).
(ii)  Pupils should conform to the ordinary reasonable demands of secondary school life (the teachers' privilege).

The pupils' privilege is the teachers' duty and the teachers' privilege is the pupils' duty. The reciprocal duties/responsibilities and privileges of pupils and teachers can be represented as in Figure 4.1.

|  | **Pupil** | **Teacher** |
|---|---|---|
| **Responsibilities** | To conform to the ordinary reasonable demands of school | (i) To educate pupils according to age, aptitude and ability <br> (ii) To treat pupils with dignity, fairness and respect |
| **Privileges** | (i) To be educated according to age, aptitude and ability <br> (ii) To be treated with dignity, fairness and respect | For the pupil to conform to the ordinary, reasonable demands of school life |

**Figure 4.1** Teacher–pupil relationships: the reciprocal nature of responsibilities and privileges

Of course the principles and tenets in the four cells of Figure 4.1 need to be 'unpacked' in order to find expression in actual teacher and pupil behaviour. This 'unpacking' may take the form of Codes of Conduct – for both pupils and teachers – and explicit curriculum differentiation to ensure that the learning needs of the full range of pupil ability is catered for and so on.

## The structure and content of educational behavioural contracts

All contracts should contain the following three essential elements:

- *responsibilities* (pupils and teachers/schools);
- *privileges* (pupils and teachers);
- *monitoring arrangements* – to ensure agreement on contract compliance/non-compliance.

In addition there are two further desirable elements: bonuses and sanctions. The 'complete' contract also contains a commencement date, a review date and freely given signatures.

### *Responsibilities*

The pupil's responsibilities will normally be academic (e.g. work output) or social (e.g. rule following behaviour). Sometimes teachers find it difficult to readily identify teacher responsibilities – thinking perhaps that something new or novel is required. In fact it is generally the case that the teachers' 'responsibilities' are activities that the teacher is already engaged in and takes for granted. However the contract *requires that the teachers' responsibilities are made explicit*. Of the many teacher responsibilities only those relevant to the task demands made of the pupil are usually included in the contract. For example, if the pupil's responsibility is to 'complete set work' then the teacher's responsibility is 'to set work' and 'to mark work': if the pupil's responsibility is to 'arrive at the lesson on time" then the teacher's responsibility is to 'start the lesson on time'.

### *Privileges*

In the mainstream school situation the major 'privilege' to be gained by a pupil is 'to attend school'. If a pupil persistently misbehaves despite the best endeavours of the school then, after due process, the pupil may be permanently excluded from school. While it is the pupil's right to continue to be educated in the school of parental choice, this is not an absolute right – it is contingent upon the pupil conforming to the ordinary, reasonable demands of the school. If this expectation of pupil behaviour is not realised then the 'right' of the pupil to be educated may be honoured by the LEA in a number of alternative ways: these include placement in a Pupil Referral Unit (PRU), Special School or the provision of home tuition.

It is the case that the 'privilege' of attending school is generally insufficient to effect appropriate change in the behaviour of a persistently difficult to manage pupil – is an insufficient motivator and positive consequence to effect change in pupil behaviour.

In the special school sector great flexibility exists to provide a range of privileges for pupils, access to the privileges being contingent on achieving and maintaining certain standards of behaviour. Free time can be made available, additional access to preferred curricular activities arranged, gift tokens to be redeemed at shops.

Some Secondary schools have adapted the type of practices referred to above and incorporated them into a whole-school approach. For example, the positive achievements monitored and recorded using the Daily Lesson Record (see Chapter 3) could be recognised by arranging subsidised school trips, awarding vouchers to be redeemed in the school tuck shop, gift tokens to be redeemed at local stores. Many schools feel, correctly, that 'public recognition' is a powerful positive consequence and consequently certificates are awarded, in the school assembly, for sustained attendance, punctuality, and the pupil behaviours monitored using the Daily Lesson Record. These positive pupil management practices are examples of informal contracting but fall short of being behavioural contracts only because they are (a) not negotiated, (b) not written down and (c) not signed by the parties concerned.

The aim of whole-school approaches to pupil management is to create a school environment in which most (ideally all) pupils behave in an appropriate manner most (ideally all) of the time. Even in the most effective schools some pupils will misbehave and continue to misbehave even when the full range of normal pupil management practices have been brought into play. It is in such cases that behavioural contracting can be used.

For pupils whose behaviour has not been influenced by normal school practices it is often the case that the privileges and sanctions available to the teachers are not powerful enough to act as effective rewards and punishments respectively. Where this is the case, home privileges, particularly pocket money and free time, can be withdrawn as a pupil 'right' and reinstated as privileges dependent on the pupil achieving certain behavioural goals in the educational situation.

### *Practical considerations*

If a pupil accepts the need to change his or her behaviour then they can be described as committed. The favoured intervention in such situations is a pupil self-management programme (see Chapter 5). Often a pupil misbehaves in school, but does not accept either that a problem exists or that there is a need to change their behaviour. Attempts can be made to elicit pupil commitment to change using the techniques of motivational interviewing (see Chapter 5). However the counselling techniques of motivational interviewing require time. For the difficult to manage pupil, sometimes, perhaps often, the possibility of exclusion from school is looming and the time required for motivational interviewing is not available. In such a situation behavioural contracting can be very effective.

The pupil's engagement in the contract is promoted by withdrawing pupil privileges – which the pupil may have seen as rights – and then reinstating the privileges incrementally as the pupil's behaviour matches standards described in the contract. The pupil may respond to the initial content of the contract by describing it as 'not fair' or in other non-accepting ways. Such a response can often be the entrée to negotiation about the content and structure of the contract: for example, the pupil can be asked why the contract is not fair, how it can be made fairer.

The pupil may move from a position of rejecting the proposed contract, through the position of discussing (negotiating) the contract and finally reach a position of accepting the contract. It could be said that initially the pupil was coerced into discussing the privileges and responsibilities contained in the contract but ultimately accepted the contract as fair and reasonable. If at all possible the pupil should have an input into the contents and structure of the contract.

Pupil input into the contract can be promoted by eliciting the pupil's view on his or her educational situation. In particular, it is helpful to identify ways in which the pupil feels that the school situation can be 'improved' from their perspective. If some of the pupil's suggestions can be accommodated, this will promote the pupil's appreciation of the 'fairness' of the process of arriving at a contract. When pupil suggestions for change cannot be accommodated, the reasons should be discussed with the pupil – an activity that communicates to the pupil that their views are important and are worthy of serious consideration. A protocol for eliciting pupil views about the school situation is presented in Figure 4.2.

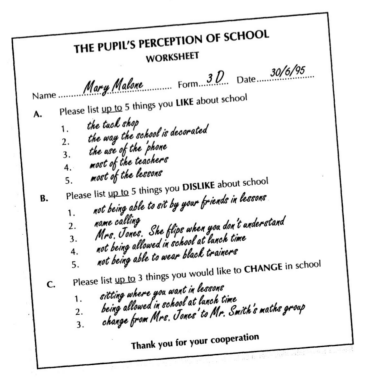

**Figure 4.2** The pupil's perception of school

**STATEMENT OF INTENT**

When I leave I want to be a nurse (or at least work in a hospital).
I realise it will help me if:

(a) I get a good reference    (b) I do my best in exams.

I want to improve my behaviour.

By this I mean pay attention in class and do the work set.

It also means behaving myself when not in lessons.

If other pupils misbehave, this is no excuse for me to misbehave.

I AM RESPONSIBLE FOR MY OWN BEHAVIOUR

Signed ...*J. South*.................................8th December 1995

**Figure 4.3** a Statement of Intent

### *The Statement of Intent*

Before the contract is signed by the parties it is important that the reasons for the pupil entering into the contract are made explicit and that the pupil's willingness is recorded. This Statement of Intent is signed by the pupil, to confirm that he or she agrees that it represents their reasons for entering into the contract. This serves to consolidate pupil commitment to the contract.

Sometimes extensive discussion precedes the agreement of the contract's structure and content and the consequent Statement of Intent may be substantial and warrant formal presentation in its own right – particularly when the pupil ultimately articulates views and propositions that support the need for behaviour change. The Statement of Intent can serve to sustain motivation to change when difficulties in contract compliance are anticipated or encountered. An example of such a free standing Statement of Intent is presented in Figure 4.3. The examples of contracts illustrated later are all prefaced with Statements of Intent.

When a behavioural contract has been drawn up it can be assessed to ascertain how near it approaches a 'textbook' contract by looking at it in the context of the following questions.

1. Is the contract prefaced by a statement of intent?
2. Are the responsibilities of *all* parties explicitly recorded?
3. Are the privileges of *all* parties recorded?
4. Does the contract contain a bonus clause (optional)?
5. Does the contract contain a sanction clause (optional)?
6. Does the contract contain a commencement date?
7. Does the contract contain a review/renegotiation date?
8. Have all parties freely signed the agreement?

## EXAMPLES OF BEHAVIOURAL CONTRACTS

There follows a number of behavioural contracts which are illustrated and commented on.

### Example 1: Attendance and punctuality (see Figure 4.4)

I wish to improve my attendance and punctuality at school.
To help me I agree to participate in the contract described below.

Signed .......... *Anthony Johns*

#### CONTRACT

**Conditions:** Anthony's £1 pocket money is to be withdrawn:

**Mr. & Mrs. Johns** agree to reinstate 15p pocket money for each day Anthony arrives at school early.

**Bonus:** 1) Anthony will receive 25p bonus if he attends school every day.

2) Anthony will receive a further 25p if he is early every day.

**Mr. Acer** agrees to send a report home with Anthony each Friday containing his attendance and punctuality record.

**Mr. & Mrs. Johns** 1) agree to pay Anthony his pocket money on Friday.

2) agree to inform Mr. Acer if Anthony is late or absent through no fault of his own – in which case Anthony will be credited with being in attendance and punctual.

This contract will be renegotiated by Anthony, Mrs. Johns, Mr. Acer and Dr. Edwards on Monday 9th April 1996 at 3.00 pm, at the school.

Signed

Anthony.............. *Anthony Johns*

Mr. & Mrs. Johns ..... *A. and C. Johns*

Mr. Acer.......... *Mr. Acer*

Dr. Edwards .......... *M. Edwards*

**Figure 4.4** Behavioural contract (example 1)

### Comments

*Pupil's responsibilities*
(a) Attend school, and
(b) Arrive on time.

Anthony's attendance at school was not a cause for particular concern, but including this as a pupil responsibility virtually ensured that at least some of the requirements of the contract would be met and therefore the teacher/pupil monitoring/review of the contract could always start on a positive note. In addition, there was little chance of Anthony losing all his pocket money because of failure to deliver his responsibilities. If the contract results in excessively negative consequences for the pupil then the possibility of the pupil unilaterally withdrawing is increased.

### Pupil's privileges
(a) 25p for each day he arrives early (he must attend to be early).
(b) 25p bonus for five days' continuous contract compliance.

As a result of punctuality being rewarded on a daily basis Anthony receives a reward even if a full week's punctual attendance is not achieved. The receipt of such a reward enhances the likelihood of Anthony remaining committed to the contract until 'flawless' compliance has been achieved.

### Teacher's responsibility
To send home each Friday a report of attendance and punctuality.

### Teacher's privilege
Anthony's regular and punctual attendance.

While the explicit reward for Anthony is reinstatement of pocket money, the teacher monitoring process creates opportunities for the supervising teacher to review progress with Anthony and provide positive social reinforcement

### Parents' responsibilities
(a) To give Anthony his pocket money on a Friday evening. Previously there was a degree of uncertainty as to when Anthony received his pocket money: this clause structured the parents' behaviour.
(b) To inform Anthony's teacher if he was late through no fault of his own.

Anthony's parents expected Anthony to get himself up for school while they slept on. Implicit in this clause was the expectation that the parents should get up with (or before) Anthony. In retrospect, the contract could have been improved by making this expectation explicit.

### Renegotiation date
This is a very important component of a behavioural contract. It may well be that during the course of a contract one of the parties feels that the contract is unfair. The knowledge of a renegotiation date enhances the probability that the discontented party will stay with the contract in the knowledge that it can be renegotiated in the near future.

## Example 2: Behaviour in school (see Figure 4.5)

Sometimes a pupil, and perhaps the pupil's parents as well, feel that the school is treating him or her unfairly. It is difficult to develop a trusting working relationship with the pupil and parent while such a view is held.

The parental perception, and perhaps even the pupil's perspective, can be changed for the better by eliciting from the pupil views as to how the school situation can be changed for the better. This can be done using the protocol illustrated earlier in Figure 4.2. Using this protocol is akin to making a statement to the pupil and parents to the effect that: 'We want to help you meet the demands of the school. In order to help you we will consider any suggestions you make which will help you feel happier in school'. Such an approach communicates to the parents the school's goodwill towards the pupil and a willingness to accommodate the pupil's wishes as far as possible. When used with Jean South (Figure 4.5) this approach resulted in the parents changing their position from 'anti-school' to 'pro-school'. The parents said to the pupil words to the effect, 'Look what the school are prepared to do to help you . . . now do your bit and behave yourself'. In this case the school agreed to Jean's request for a change of tutor group.

**AGREEMENT**

I want to improve my behaviour at school
To help me I agree to enter into the contract described below:

Signed.......*Jean South*.......................

**The School's Commitments**
1. **Mrs. Dutch agrees:**
   a) To change Jean's tutor group
   b) To arrange a 'career interview' for Jean
   c) To make herself available to Jean so that Jean may discuss any problems she has.

2. **Miss Foot agrees:**
   To rate Jean's report card daily as satisfactory or unsatisfactory

**The Parents' Commitments**

**Mr. & Mrs. South agree:**
   a) To give Jean 20p pocket money on each occasion a 'satisfactory' rating is obtained.
   b) To give Jean a bonus of 50p pocket money if she receives 5 'satisfactory' ratings in a week.
   c) To take Jean to the Club on Friday and Sunday nights if no major disruptive incident at school is reported.

**Jean's Commitments**
   a) To have her report card signed at each lesson.
   b) To take home the Home/School Report Card daily.

**Sanctions**
1. If Jean is engaged in a major disruptive incident then:
   a) for each major disruptive incident Jean will not accompany her parents to the Club on one night
   b) Jean will be suspended from school with parental consent.

2. If Jean is involved in minor disruptive incidents she may be individually time tabled by Mrs. Dutch.
   If Jean forgets her Report Card then she will automatically receive an 'unsatisfactory' rating.

This agreement will be reviewed on Monday 8th December at 3.35 pm.

Signed   Jean South .......*J. South*....... Signed .......*C. Dutch*.......Mrs Dutch

Signed   Mrs. South .......*A. South*....... Signed .......*J. Foot*.......Mrs. Foot

**Figure 4.5** Behavioural contract (example 2)

Jean could occasionally be very disruptive in school: therefore in addition to reinstating pocket money for 'satisfactory' ratings of behaviour, a treat – taking Jean to a Social Club – was made dependent on the non occurrence of disruptive behaviour. A 'heavy' sanction was also agreed if a major disruptive incident occurred – exclusion from school. At the beginning of discussions about Jean's behaviour the parents were adamantly opposed to the possibility of school exclusion but at the end of the contract negotiation they were prepared to accept it: for they viewed the whole process of negotiating the contract as an attempt to help Jean and they judged the possible suspension of Jean as 'fair'.

### Example 3: Behaviour in a specific curriculum area (see Figure 4.6)

*Comments.* This contract combines an on-report protocol with a behavioural contract. The contract is illustrated in Figure 4.6 and the monitoring dimension of the contract is the on-report protocol illustrated in Figure 4.7.

The contract was aimed at improving pupil effort and behaviour in one problematic lesson, English. It would obviously be an inefficient strategy to require all subject teachers to monitor behaviour in all lessons when concern is expressed in the English class alone.

The effectiveness of the behavioural contract can be evaluated by reviewing the data over a number of weeks. For example the effectiveness of the contract illustrated in Figure 4.6 can be evaluated by reviewing the record of achievement presented in Figure 4.8.

### Example 4: Attendance, punctuality and behaviour in lessons (see Figure 4.9)

*Comments.* This contract is similar in style to the contract described in Example 3. The obvious differences are that three behaviours, not one, are targeted and because of this two Record (monitoring) Cards are used. These are illustrated in Figures 4.10 and 4.11. The fact that the pupil carries the Record Cards around with them, promotes contract compliance in two ways: (a) by acting as a 'reminder' (cue) about the behaviour standards required to receive the rewards, and (b) as a cue to self-reinforcement when the record of the ongoing pocket money earned is read.

When the rationale of contracting is not understood, it is easy to slip into ineffective practices. For example, the 'Proclamation' illustrated in Figure 4.12 was erroneously presented to parents as a contract. This 'contract':

(a) Makes no reference to the school's responsibilities.
(b) Sets idealistic, over generalised standards of behaviour – it is difficult to identify either the specific behaviours of concern or the corresponding desired behaviours.
(c) Makes vague demands of the pupil – 'acceptable manner', 'to the appropriate standard', 'all arrangements that apply'.
(d) Sets a vague criteria for the only consequence that is made explicit – 'anything of a serious nature'.

(e) Fudges accountability/responsibility for the consequence – 'I will be expected'.

(f) Fails to recognise parental rights to challenge school exclusions by coercing parents to 'voluntarily' withdraw their child from school.

(g) Is unrealistic in the time scale of the task demands – 'at any future date'.

(h) Was not arrived at as a product of negotiation.

Other important comments to note are:

(a) A cynic might suggest that the purpose of the 'contract' illustrated in Figure 4.12 was not to help the pupil change his or her behaviour to meet the standards necessary to remain a pupil at the school but to 'ease' the pupil out of the school with the minimum of fuss or inconvenience.

(b) A contract is only a piece of paper: how can a piece of paper change the behaviour of a pupil? The answer is that it cannot. It is not the contract per se which is of crucial importance but the process *of arriving at the contract*. Negotiating a contract should not be a mechanistic process: the relationships, attitudes, commitments, unconditional positive regard for the pupil are all significant aspects of the process.

(c) Behavioural contracts are a reactive response to inappropriate pupil behaviour. Proactive management initiatives to prevent the occurrence of inappropriate pupil behaviour are a preferred modus operandi. Reference has been made earlier in the chapter to using an on-report protocol in a proactive way. In an analogous manner the rationale and practice of behavioural contracting can be used proactively. Examples of one such School–Pupil Agreement are described in the following section.

I wish to move up into a higher class.

To help me I wish to improve:

(1) My 'effort' in English lessons. (2) My 'effort' with English homework.

I therefore agree to participate in the contract described below.

Signed .......... *Robert Wright* ..........

**CONDITIONS:**

Robert's pocket money will be *withdrawn*

**MRS. WRIGHT agrees:**

(a) to reinstate *10p* for each English lesson in which 'effort' is recorded as *a or b;*

(b) to reinstate a further *10p* for each English homework which receives a mark of *1 or 2.*

**BONUS:**

At the end of each week:

(1) Robert will receive a further *25p* bonus if his 'effort' in *All 6* English lessons has been recorded as *a or b;*

(2) Robert will receive a further *20p* bonus if both English homeworks received a mark of *1 or 2.*

**MRS. YEARHEAD agrees:**

(a) to discuss the marks with Robert before recording them on his Record Card;

(b) to note on the Record Card if Robert was not given any English homework on a certain night – in which case he will be credited with a satisfactory mark, i.e. 1;

(c) to send the Record Card home each Friday, containing a record of his effort in class and homework marks and the amount of pocket money earned.

**MRS. WRIGHT agrees:**

(1) to pay Robert his pocket money each *Saturday;*

(2) to return the weekly Record Card to Mrs. Yearhead on Monday;

(3) to inform Mrs. Yearhead if Robert is unable to do his homework, through no fault of his own – in which case he will be credited with a satisfactory mark, i.e. 1.

This contract will be renegotiated by Robert, Mrs. Wright, Mrs. Yearhead and Mrs. Bradshaw on *Friday 27th October* at *3.15 pm* at the school.

Signed:

Robert Wright........... *Robert Wright* ...........   Mrs. Yearhead........... *A. Yearhead* ...........

Mrs. Wright ........... *B. Wright* ...........   Mrs. Bradshaw........... *A. Bradshaw* ...........

**Figure 4.6** Behavioural contract (example 3)

## RECORD CARD

Name.......... *Robert Wright* ..........          Week beginning .......... *7.9.95* ..........

|  | MONDAY | TUESDAY | WEDNESDAY | THURSDAY | FRIDAY |  |
|---|---|---|---|---|---|---|
| 'Effort' in English * Lessons A - D | *A* | *A* | *B* *B* | *A* | *A* |  |
| English Homework ** 1 - 4 | / | *2* | / | / | *2* | **TOTAL** |
| Pocket Money Earned | *10p* | *20p* | *20p* | *10p* | *20p* | *80p* |

* A — Very Good
  B — Good
  C — Average
  D — Poor

** 1 — Complete and totally correct
   2 — Complete and largely correct
   3 — Complete but largely incorrect
   4 — Incomplete

| BONUS | *45p* |
|---|---|
| TOTAL | *£1.25* |

**Figure 4.7** Monitoring record of pupil responsibilities and privileges

| DAY | MONDAY | TUESDAY | | WEDNESDAY | | THURSDAY | FRIDAY | | POCKET MONEY EARNED |
|---|---|---|---|---|---|---|---|---|---|
| **INTERVENTION DATA** | | | | | | | | | |
| **Effort in English** | *Lesson | *Lesson | **Home-work | *Lesson | *Lesson | *Lesson | *Lesson | **Home-work | |
| Week 1 | A | A | 2 | B | B | A | A | 2 | £1.25 |
| Week 2 | A | A | 1 | A | A | B | B | 2 | £1.25 |
| Week 3 | Absent Credited B | Absent Credited B | 2 | A | A | A | A | 3 | 95p |
| Week 4 | A | A | 2 | A | A | A | B | 2 | £1.25 |
| Week 5 | A | A | 2 | B | B | A | A | 2 | £1.25 |

```
* A — Very Good          ** 1 — Complete and totally correct
  B — Good                  2 — Complete and largely correct
  C — Average               3 — Complete but largely incorrect
  D — Poor                  4 — Incomplete
```

**Figure 4.8** Evaluation of a behavioural contract

I am in my last year at school and am looking forward to leaving and to getting a job. So that my employers will get a better report from school, I wish to improve my attendance, punctuality and behaviour in class. To help me, I agree to participate in the contract described below:

Signed *Austen Elliot*

**CONDITIONS:** Austen's pocket money will be withdrawn **but**
Austen's possible pocket money will be *increased from £2.50 to £3.50.*

**MRS. ELLIOT** agrees:
(a) to reinstate *20p* for each full day Austen attends school;
(b) to reinstate a further *10p* for each day that Austen arrives at school by *9.00 am* in the morning, and by *1.30 pm* in the afternoon;
(c) to reinstate a further *10p* for each day that Austen's behaviour has been *satisfactory* in *at least 6* out of the *7* lessons.

**BONUS:**
At the end of each week:
(1) Austen will receive a *50p* bonus if he has attended school for 5 full days;
(2) Austen will receive a further *50p* bonus if he has arrived by 9.00 am every morning, and by *1.30 pm* every afternoon;
(3) Austen will receive a further *50p* bonus if his behaviur has never been less than *satisfactory.*

**MISS BOLTON** agrees to send the Record Card home each Friday, containing a record of his attendance, punctuality and behaviour, and the amount of pocket money earned.

**MRS. ELLIOT** agrees:
(1) to pay Austen his pocket money each *Friday night;*
(2) to return the weekly Record Card to Miss Bolton on Monday;
(3) to inform Miss Bolton if Austen is absent or late, through no fault of his own, in which case he will be credited with being in attendance and punctual.

This contract would be renegotiated by Austen, Mrs. Elliot, Miss Bolton and Mrs. Bradshaw on *Friday 5th November 1995* at *3.00 pm* at the school.

Signed:  Austen Elliot *Austen Elliot*      Mrs. Elliot *S. Elliot*

Miss Bolton *B. Bolton*      Mrs. Bradshaw *J. Bradshaw*

**Figure 4.9** Behavioural contract (example 4)

| Name *Austen Elliot* | | Week beginning *Monday, 25th October, 1995* | | | |
|---|---|---|---|---|---|
| Please sign in the appropriate cell if Austen's behaviour has been *Satisfactory* in your lesson | | | | | |
| LESSON | MONDAY | TUESDAY | WEDNESDAY | THURSDAY | FRIDAY | |
| 1 | Satisfactory | Satisfactory | Satisfactory | Satisfactory | Satisfactory | |
| 2 | Satisfactory | Satisfactory | Satisfactory | Satisfactory | Satisfactory | |
| 3 | Satisfactory | Satisfactory | Satisfactory | Satisfactory | Satisfactory | |
| 4 | Satisfactory | Satisfactory | Satisfactory | Satisfactory | Satisfactory | |
| 5 | Satisfactory | Satisfactory | Satisfactory | Satisfactory | Satisfactory | |
| 6 | Satisfactory | Satisfactory | Satisfactory | Satisfactory | Satisfactory | |
| 7 | Satisfactory | Satisfactory | Satisfactory | Satisfactory | Satisfactory | TOTALS |
| Bonus Earned | 10p | 10p | 10p | 10p | 10p | 50p |
| 50p | | | | GRAND TOTAL | | £1.00 |

**Figure 4.10** Behavioural record (satisfactory/not satisfactory)

## RECORD CARD

| Name *Austen Elliot* | | | | Week beginning | | | | *25/10/95* | | |
|---|---|---|---|---|---|---|---|---|---|---|
| | MONDAY | | TUESDAY | | WEDNESDAY | | THURSDAY | | FRIDAY | |
| | A or P | Time of Arrival | A or P | Time of Arrival | A or P | Time of Arrival | A or P | Time of Arrival | A or P | Time of Arrival | |
| Morning | P | 8.50 am | P | 8.55 am | P | 8.49 am | P | 8.44 am | P | 8.58 am | |
| Afternoon | P | 1.28 pm | P | 1.25 pm | P | 1.27 pm | P | 1.25 pm | P | 1.29 pm | TOTAL |
| Pocket Money Earned | 20p 10p | | 20p 10p | | 20p 10p | | 20p 10p | | 20p 10p | | £1.50 |
| * A or P = Absent or Present | | | | | | | | BONUS | | £1 |
| | | | | | | | | GRAND TOTAL | | £2.50 |

**Figure 4.11** Attendance and punctuality record

I,.................................... ..............................agree that I will:

1. attend regularly and punctually

2. obey all school rules

3. behave in an acceptable manner in lessons

4. act with courtesy towards members of staff

5. cooperate with members of staff and other pupils

6. complete all necessary class and homework tasks to the appropriate standard

7. obey all the lunchtime arrangements that apply and understand and accept that if anything of a serious nature occurs at a future date, I will be expected to continue my education at another school.

Signed ................................. (pupil)

................................. (parent)

................................. (home tutor)

................................. (head/deputy head)

................................. (governor)

Date ...................................

**Figure 4.12** A Proclamation 'masquerading' as a contract

## SCHOOL–PUPIL CONTRACTS

### School–Pupil Agreement (example 1)

An amalgamated Secondary Modern and Grammar School decided that the Prefect system was 'elitist' in that a small number of fifth formers were selected to join the school staff in monitoring/controlling the behaviour of the rest of the pupils. It was felt that all Year 11 pupils should have the opportunity of becoming prefects – for such a situation would be indicative of the pupil's commitment to the aims, ideals and behavioural standards of the school.

At the beginning of the Summer term all fourth year pupils were invited to apply for Senior Pupil (Prefect) status and to receive a Senior Pupil Card. The Application Form is illustrated in Figure 4.13. This application is analogous to a Statement of Intent and all applications are accepted in good faith. Rarely do more than a handful of pupils fail to apply.

Before being given the opportunity to apply for Senior Pupil status the responsibilities of the position are made known to the Year 10 pupils by the form tutors. The guidance given to form tutors in addressing the form groups is set out overleaf.

## APPLICATION FOR A SENIOR PUPIL CARD

NAME (Block Letters) . . . . . . . . . . . . . . . .  FORM . . . . . . . . . .

I wish to apply for a Senior Pupil Card.

I realise that as a Senior Pupil I will be expected to assist in the running of the school, and to conform to the rules of the school, its Code of Conduct and Dress and to encourage, by deed and example, the rest of the school to observe them.  I also realise that if I fail to live up to this undertaking my card can be endorsed or withdrawn and I will lose the privileges associated with being a Senior Pupil.

Signed . . . . . . . . . . . . . . . . . . . . . . . . .

Date . . . . . . . . . . . . . . . . . . . . . . . .

**Figure 4.13** Application for Senior Pupil Card

*To Form Tutors Year 10*
*The following is offered as guidance in recruiting volunteers for Senior Pupil Status prior to organising duty teams.*

On Monday, Form Tutors will ask for volunteers from their Form to make up the Form Duty Teams. I hope we will, as last year, have plenty of volunteers prepared to do a good job. Ideally we would like all pupils to volunteer (in which case each Form will have two duty teams).

*Note 1* (to be brought to the attention of all pupils).

**Don't volunteer** – if what you wear bears little resemblance to our school uniform. We cannot have pupils on duty who set a bad example in their dress to the younger pupils.

**Don't volunteer** – if you need a member of staff with you to make sure you don't get into trouble. In other words you feel you are not yet mature enough to act sensibly.

**Don't volunteer** – if you are not prepared to stay for dinner on your duty day, as part of your duty will be at dinner time.

**Don't volunteer** – if you are frequently absent from school, or late. You will let your Duty Team down.

*Note 2* (*to be emphasised* – and *remind pupils* that Senior Pupil Status will be recorded in their Record of Achievements).

**Volunteer** – if you want to help to support an orderly school by helping younger pupils behave responsibly.

**Volunteer** – if you want to take on real responsibility in helping to run the school.

**Volunteer** – if you feel you are mature enough to take on this real responsibility.

*What do you get in return?*

1. The opportunity to serve the school and gain experience through taking on new, important responsibilities.

2. When the present Year 11 have left and GCSE examinations are over, if they have done their job well and shown a sense of responsibility the Duty Teams will be allowed to use Room T5 as a Social Centre/Common Room, where they can relax, make coffee and listen to music. This privilege will eventually be extended to all those in next year's Fifth who choose to continue to be Senior Pupils.

*Senior Pupil privileges*

1. Senior Pupils are allowed to use the Fifth Year Common Room at any time when not required for lessons or Senior Pupil duties.

2. Coffee making facilities will be made available and music (not too loud!) may be played.

3. Holders of a Senior Pupil Card also have right of entrance to the weekly Upper School Disco.

The holders of a Senior Pupil Card could have an 'endorsement' if they were behaving in an inappropriate manner. Consultation with the pupils indicated that the Senior Pupil Card System was well received – but some pupils felt teachers were inconsistent when dispensing endorsements. A staff review of this matter was seen as 'fine tuning' the system.

A Year 11 Council was also established – consisting of two elected members from each of the eight tutor groups. The Council (chaired by a Year 11 Form Tutor) helped arrange and organise the discos and refreshments in the Fifth Year Common Room. In addition the Council considered the reinstatement of Senior Pupil Cards – for three endorsements resulted in automatic loss of Senior Pupil status.

## School–Pupil Agreement (example 2)

The second example (Figure 4.14) of a School–Pupil Agreement is from a school catering for pupils experiencing emotional/behavioural difficulties (EBD).

# OBELISK SCHOOL

## AIMS OF LEAVERS DEPARTMENT

1) To develop, within each pupil, responsibility for his/her own actions.
2) To prepare pupils for the transition from school to employment and/or college.
3) To provide as broad a curriculum, academically, practically and physically, as possible.
4) To foster, and provide, opportunities for academic achievement at appropriate levels.
5) To encourage harmonious working relationships between pupils and between pupils and staff based on respect for the needs and failings of others.
6) To develop an awareness of the wider community beyond school and an appreciation of the needs and problems of others.

## STUDENT PRIVILEGES – SCHOOL RESPONSIBILITIES

### CURRICULUM

1) Opportunity to take terminal examinations at Key Stage 4 of the National Curriculum in:
   1) Maths
   2) English
   3) C.D.T. (Design and Realisation or Technology)
   4) Art and Design
   5) Science
2) Opportunity to complete stages of the S.M.P. (11–16) Graduated Assessment Scheme.
3) Opportunity to acquire A.E.B. Basic Skills Certificates in Graphicacy and Science, Statements of Achievement in Graphicacy, Information Technology, Science, History and Geography.
4) Opportunity to acquire Statements of Achievement and Letters of Credit under the N.P.R.A. Unit Accreditation Scheme within the Modular Curriculum, operating one morning per week:

   Community Service, e.g. Infant School, Special School, Residential Home.

   Community Studies, e.g. Study of Vandalism

   Practical Life Skills, e.g. Painting and Decorating, Health-related Fitness.

   Cross-Curricular Activities, e.g. Producing School Newspaper, Planning a Holiday.

   Money Management, e.g. Personal Budgeting, Introduction to Bank Services.
5) Opportunity to undertake a two-week work experience placement.
6) Opportunity to participate in annual school camp and outdoor pursuits activities.
7) Opportunity to continue Personal and Social Education through Careers Education, Preparation for Parenthood and Sex Education.

All Fifth Years will receive a Record of their Achievements in the aforementioned areas.

The curriculum will be continually developed in line with the National Curriculum and to take advantage of local facilities, e.g. F.E. College Open Courses and Y.T.S. links in order that both academic and personal development are maximised.

**Figure 4.14** School–Pupil Agreement from a school catering for pupils with emotional/behavioural difficulties

## STUDENT RESPONSIBILITIES – TEACHER PRIVILEGES

1) Regular attendance.

2) Willingness and commitment to take advantage of the curricular opportunities available. This may require use of the option system to achieve personal success.

3) A recognition of the needs of all other members of a teaching group as well as their own personal choices.

4) A willingness to comply with reasonable requests from staff in order that the needs and expectations of the teaching group can be met.

**All Parties accept that**

students who are unwilling to follow the guidelines set out above are denying themselves and the others in the group the opportunity to take advantage of the leavers' curriculum.

At this late stage in their school career responsibility for actions must rest largely within the individual. In the event that a student does not accept this responsibility the usual school procedures for dealing with unacceptable behaviour, Time Out, Token Strategies, Compulsory Lessons, will apply.

In extreme cases, however, it may be deemed appropriate to pursue a course of temporary exclusion for the rest of the day. A decision of this nature will be taken by a senior member of staff in consultation with members of staff concerned and parents will be notified.

All parties agree that the above procedure is fair and reasonable and designed to protect both the individual student and other members of the group.

Student Signature ................................................ Date ..............................

Parent/Guardian Signature ............................................. Date...............................

Head Teacher Signature ................................................ Date ..............................

Arrangements for sending home

........................................................................................................................

........................................................................................................................

**Figure 4.14 cont.**

## HOME–SCHOOL CONTRACTS

### School–Parent Agreements

In 1998 the Government issued Guidance on home–school agreements. Such agreements involved both school and parents/carers signing an agreement. This agreement must contain a description of:

(i)    the school's aims, expectations and values;
(ii)   the school's responsibilities to the pupil; and
(iii)  the parents' responsibilities.

The aim of the home–school agreement is to promote a positive working relationship between parents/carers and school. These agreements are offered to all parents and are identical for all. However when an individual pupil's behaviour is particularly problematic a particular home–school contract or agreement can be drawn up to address the particular difficulties that the pupil experiences. Such an agreement is presented as Figure 4.15.

## CONTRACT OF LAST RESORT

### Sustaining class teacher involvement in pupil management after lesson exclusion

Sometimes a pupil will persist in engaging in challenging behaviour despite the positive pupil management practices described in this book. In such a situation the possibility exists that the pupil will be referred for placement in an alternative, perhaps more specialised educational environment, e.g. a Pupil Referral Unit or even a Special School. The suggestion of such a course of action is often not well received by the pupil who may make protestations and commitments to behave appropriately. While the proposed course of action is put into effect, a 'final' attempt can be made to capitalise on the pupil's wish to continue his or her education at the present school. This is effected in the following way.

The pupil is interviewed by the teacher whose authority is persistently challenged by the pupil. A senior member of staff (Head of Year, Head of Department, Deputy headteacher) is present at the interview but adopts a somewhat passive role – his or her presence is primarily required to act as a 'witness'. The teacher:

(a) Describes in explicit terms the pupil behaviours giving concern.
(b) States clearly and precisely that these behaviours are totally unacceptable and must stop.
(c) Invites the pupil to respond to the school's concern and assures the pupil that their views will be considered and responded to.
(d) Presents the pupil with a pre-prepared written Statement of Intent which declares the pupil's intention not to engage in the inappropriate behaviours.
(e) Invites the pupil to sign the Statement of Intent.

This Statement of Intent is not a contract and there is no negotiation component (this will have been tried previously and not produced sustained change in pupil behaviour). The school is assertively setting behavioural limits and indicating to the pupil that continued attendance at school is conditional on the pupil's behaviour staying within the limits.

# HOME – SCHOOL CONTRACTS (School – Parent Agreements)

## PARENT

1)   We accept that as *Tom's* parents we share responsibility for his/her behaviour in school with the teachers and with *Tom* himself/herself.

2)   We have received a copy of the school brochure and we will do our utmost to assist the school in achieving the aims contained in the brochure. We agree to support the school by ensuring that *Tom* conforms to the school rules. Should the school request support we agree to cooperate with any home/school strategy suggested by the school.

3)   We understand that we will be invited to Parents' Evenings which are held during the Autumn and Summer terms. In addition, we are aware that should we visit to discuss *Tom's* progress at any time during the year then, providing the school is given sufficient notice, arrangements will be made to see *Tom's* teachers.

4)   We understand that *Tom's* Statement of Special Educational Need will be reviewed annually and that we will be invited to contribute to the review.

## SCHOOL

1)   We accept that as *Tom's* teachers we take responsibility for his/her academic and social development and share responsibility for his/her behaviour with his/her parents.

2)   At the parents' request we will do our utmost to help *Tom* to conform to socially acceptable behaviour at home.

3)   We promise to ensure that *Tom's* parents are informed of any changes in behaviour that we consider necessary to inform you of.

4)   In addition to any other information regarding *Tom's* progress, the School will provide a written report at the end of the academic year.

5)   We will arrange two Parents' Evenings per year and invite *Tom's* parents. In addition, we will make the necessary arrangements for *Tom's* parents to visit the school and discuss progress on demand: given sufficient notice all appropriate teachers will be available for consultation.

SIGNED    *Mrs. S. Jones*
.................................................................    PARENT

*Tom Jones*
.................................................................    PUPIL

*John Baker*
.................................................................    HEADMASTER

**Figure 4.15** An example of a School–Parent Agreement

(f) The teacher explains to the pupil the course of action to be followed if the pupil engages in the unacceptable behaviour, namely

- the incident will be recorded by the teacher involved and the description will be signed by the pupil (this is known as a notification)
- the pupil can 'resubmit' a Statement of Intent and if three consecutive lessons without a further notification are achieved then the original notification is cancelled
- if a second notification is recorded the pupil is immediately asked to leave the lesson and go to a predetermined place (which is supervised).

(g) A meeting is convened as soon after the second notification as possible. The meeting is chaired and conducted by the Senior teacher who witnessed the first Statement of Intent. The teacher who was the 'recipient' of the disruptive behaviours (who probably chaired/conducted the first meeting) attends the second meeting.

(h) The pupil's educational situation is reviewed and the further increased concern of the school is communicated to the pupil.

(i) The pupil is invited to sign a further pre-prepared Statement of Intent.

### *Parental involvement*

It may be that when concern about pupil behaviour, i.e. lack of success of positive pupil management interventions, has necessitated the school resorting to the foregoing somewhat negatively biased response, parental involvement and cooperation will have already been sought. However, it is essential to involve parents further and brief them if this strategy is to be embarked upon.

An example of a pre-prepared Statement of Intent is illustrated in Figure 4.16 and an example of a Statement of Intent to be witnessed by the parents is illustrated in Figure 4.17.

## CONCLUDING OBSERVATIONS

In December 1993 the Department for Education released six Draft Circulars on 'Pupils with Problems'. Circular 1, 'Pupil Behaviour and Discipline' is supportive of the use of behavioural contracts – although this term is not used. For example, the following appears:

a plan of action (preferably in writing and signed by those present)

The requirements of this 'plan of action' appear consistent with the requirements of a behavioural contract: it is probably the case that the term 'contract' was not used because it has connotations of a legally binding agreement – which it is not. Elsewhere the Draft Circular also commends the practice of home–school agreements:

Such agreements (home–school agreements), which specify the expectations of pupils, parents and the school

## LEAFY PARK HIGH SCHOOL STANDARDS OF BEHAVIOUR

**PURPOSE**

The purpose of this document is to describe, in writing, certain behaviours which are totally unacceptable and will not be permitted in Leafy Park High School. The behaviours are:

1. REFUSING TO OBEY THE TEACHERS' REQUESTS.
2. ANSWERING THE TEACHER IN A CHEEKY OR AGRESSIVE MANNER.
3. THE USE OF RUDE LANGUAGE.

You are invited to sign an agreement stating that you will not engage in these behaviours.

This is an agreement between........................................ and my teachers at Leafy Park High School.

I agree that I have seriously misbehaved in some of my French lessons. I intend to improve my behaviour. I will sign my name to show my teachers that I recognise the importance of this agreement.

If I break this agreement, my teacher will give me a chance to try again but the incident will be written down in a book. This is a **Notification** I will have to accept a punishment. When I behave for three successive lessons the **Notification** will be removed from the book.

If I have two notifications written down I will have to meet my teachers again. A senior teacher will conduct a new meeting and my parents will be informed about my behaviour. I will be invited to make a new agreement, more serious consequences will result if I do not keep the agreement.

I........................... have read this statement and understand what it means.

I........................... intend to stop behaving in the following ways:

1. Defiantly, verbally or otherwise, refuse to obey my teachers.
2. Answering back in a cheeky or agressive manner.
3. Using rude language.

Signed..................................................

Signed.................................................. Pupil

Teacher     Date.....................

**Figure 4.16** Prepared Statement of Intent

Perhaps a shortcoming of the Circular is the lack of emphasis given to the benefits of the school making the school's responsibilities explicit to the parents, for an undue focus on the pupil's/parent's responsibilities alone can lead to feelings of unfairness, victimisation and alienation on the part of the pupil and/or the parents.

The practice of home–school agreements has a successful history in the Special Education Sector. The essential requirement of such agreements is that they are seen as fair, balanced and indicative that the school's purpose is to serve the pupil. Such a 'flavour' to the agreement is apt to elicit support and goodwill from parents.

## MY STATEMENT OF INTENT

**I INTEND TO IMPROVE MY BEHAVIOUR DURING MY FRENCH LESSONS.**

### IN ORDER TO ACHIEVE THIS I PROMISE TO:

1. Enter the room quietly and sensibly.
2. Go straight to my place.
3. Get out my books and writing equipment and wait my next instruction.
4. Raise my hand for teacher attention.
5. Talk only about my work.
6. Stay in my place until the teacher grants me permission to move.
7. Try and complete my set tasks.
8. Leave the room quietly and sensibly under the direction of my teacher.

### I WILL NOT:

1. Defiantly (verbally or otherwise) refuse to follow teachers' instructions.
2. Answer teachers in an agressive or cheeky manner.
3. Use rude language or disturb other pupils.

Signing this statement of intent signifies that I am going to try very hard to keep all these promises. I will show this card to my parents and obtain their signature to show that they are also aware of my intentions.

Pupil Signature .........................................

Parent Signature ......................................... Date ....................

**Figure 4.17** Statement of Intent (Parental Information)

# CHAPTER 5

# Pupil self-management

The aims of this chapter are to:

(i) Present a rationale for pupil self-management.
(ii) Describe a model of the self-regulation of behaviour.
(iii) Explain the reactivity of self-recording.
(iv) Present guidelines for

- commitment to self-monitoring
- successful self-monitoring.

(v) Describe protocols for

- pupil self-management
- pupil-teacher monitoring.

## RATIONALE

The on-report system (see Chapter 3) is designed to bring pupil behaviour under teacher control; it thus constitutes a method of reducing inappropriate pupil behaviour and increasing appropriate behaviour. While appropriate behaviour achieved in this manner is desirable, it is nonetheless teacher controlled. Ideally pupil behaviour should be under pupil self-control, i.e. appropriate behaviour should also be responsible behaviour.

*Responsible behaviour* is appropriate behaviour which occurs in the absence of teachers – it is not teacher dependent as it is pupil self-motivated. This concept of a continuum of control is illustrated in Figure 5.1.

Sometimes when a pupil is confronted with their misdemeanour they make protestations of their intent 'to behave', i.e. to conform to the ordinary demands of school life (attend on time, complete homework, not insult teachers). However it is not uncommon for the very same pupil to be referred again to the pastoral teacher within a few days of the first referral – despite the pupil's previous commitments 'to behave'. Such situations might give rise to the pupil being described as insincere, dishonest or expedient – the lack of pupil behaviour change being interpreted as indicating a lack of commitment to change. This may well be the case, and an appropriate response might be to place the pupil on-report (see Chapter 3) or to negotiate a contract (see Chapter 4). However it may be that the pupil's protestations to change were honest and sincere, and the lack of change may be a consequence of lack of self-control or will-power. Consequently, if the pupil can be helped to change his or her behaviour then they will have been helped to acquire self-control or will-dower.

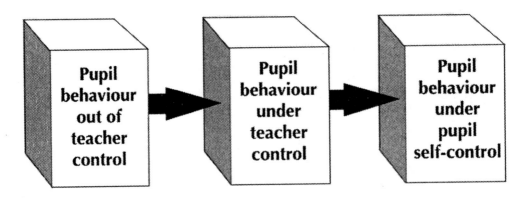

**Figure 5.1** The continuum of control

Looked at in this way *self-control* is viewed as the ability to change one's own behaviour. Thus to help a pupil to change his or her behaviour is to help the pupil acquire self-control by exercising *will-power.*

This is a somewhat novel concept of 'will-power' and contrasts with the more traditional personality trait approach. Within the trait theory approach, if a pupil misbehaves and fails to effect appropriate behaviour change the problem analysis may be that the pupil lacks self-control or will-power: if will-power is conceptualised as a personality trait and is therefore seen as substantially unchangeable, then the problem analysis is pessimistic to the extent that it could be summarised as follows:

- the problem behaviours occur because the pupil lacks will-power
- will-power is a personality trait
- personality traits are substantially constant, i.e. not susceptible to change
- therefore nothing can be done about the problem.

In contrast behavioural psychologists conceptualise will-power in operational terms which are functionally useful because behaviour change is facilitated. Thus if a pupil loses their temper because they lack self-control and the pupil is helped to acquire anger control strategies, then it can be argued that the pupil has been helped to acquire self-control, i.e. lack of self-control is conceptualised as a skill deficit which is behaviour (and even situation) specific. Skills can be taught/learnt and therefore self-control/will-power can be taught/learnt.

## THE SELF-REGULATION OF BEHAVIOUR

Effecting change in pupil behaviour using strategies derived from a consideration of the model of the self-regulation of behaviour is more effectively achieved if the rationale underlying the practices is understood. The main strategies used are a range of variants of the practice of self-monitoring and an appreciation of the theoretical framework of self-regulation enhances the effectiveness of self-monitoring strategies.

## A theoretical framework of self-regulation

Everyday activities are usually carried out at the automatic level, i.e. they are not made up of a series of conscious, discrete acts which require continuous decisions about alternatives. An example of such an everyday activity carried out at the automatic level would be driving a car. However, when everyday activities carried out at the automatic level cease to achieve the intended outcome, then the individual has to consciously consider his or her behaviour – and a conscious self-regulation process will begin.

### *Self-monitoring*

The first stage in the self-regulation of behaviour is self-monitoring or self-observation. This stage involves deliberately and carefully attending to one's own behaviour.

### *Self-evaluation*

The second stage of the self-regulation of behaviour is the self-evaluation process. When a person behaves, they have a performance standard/criterion/ goal to which they aspire. The second stage of the process consists of a comparison being made between the information obtained from self-monitoring and the self-set criterion for the given behaviour. This is the self-evaluation stage.

### *Self-reinforcement*

The third stage of the self-regulation of behaviour consists of self-reinforcement – contingent upon the degree to which the actual behaviour approximates to, matches, or deviates from, the performance standard or criterion, i.e. from the intended behaviour. If the behaviour matches the standard, then this information constitutes positive feedback and positive self-reinforcement should result in the 'strength' of the behaviour being increased. If the behaviour does not meet the standard set, then this information constitutes negative feedback. The effect of this negative feedback on the individual may be that

– *behaviour change is attempted,* self-monitored and self-evaluated: if the standard is achieved then the strength of the behaviour is increased; if the standard is not achieved then this process is repeated until the performance approximates to or matches the standard; or
– the person *gives up trying* to achieve the behaviour standard or criterion.

This third stage can be considered a motivational process: for the achievement of self-set criteria or standards can act as a motivator (or at least reinforce existing motivation) to continue the behaviour, i.e. standard (goal) achievement acts as a reinforcing consequence. This model of the self-regulation of behaviour is illustrated in Figure 5.2. It is pivotal to the practices of self-management.

*Self-management practices.* Self-management programmes can involve standard setting, self-monitoring and self-reinforcement. In educational settings it is the practices of goal (standard) setting, and self-monitoring which are emphasised in pupil self-management programmes.

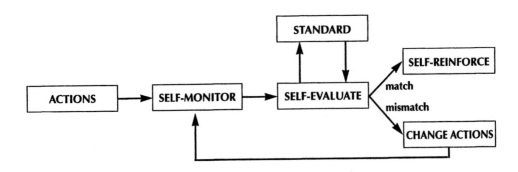

**Figure 5.2** Model of self-regulation of behaviour

Self-management practices are most easily implemented when the pupil is concerned about his or her problems and wishes to resolve them. If a pupil is not committed to change then the teacher may:

- implement a teacher determined pupil management programme, e.g. 'on-report'; or
- negotiate a behavioural contract; or
- engage in motivational interviewing (see Chapter 7).

*Role of the teacher.* This is wide ranging and includes:

(a) Eliciting and supporting the pupil's view that behaviour change is possible and desirable.
(b) Indicating the limitations of the teacher's role.
(c) Communicating the expectation that the pupil will
   - carry out the exercises associated with the programme
   - take responsibility for initiating and maintaining behaviour change.
(d) Indicating that the teacher will be available to
   - teach the pupil techniques that make change easier
   - provide guidance in formulating the change programme.
(e) Informing the pupil about the nature of self-management programmes and providing support (positive reinforcement) to the pupil during the course of the programme.

*Self-monitoring.* Traditional behaviour modification programmes involve the observing and recording of behaviour by an independent observer to obtain a baseline measure prior to the introduction of a management programme. When a person decides to change his or her own behaviour it can be conceptualised as self behaviour modification. As with any behaviour modification (BM) programme the first step involves the identification of the behaviour(s) to be changed. In educational situations concern about pupil behaviour is commonly brought to the pupil's attention by a teacher, e.g. poor time-keeping, failure to complete homework, arguing with the teacher, non-compliance. The second step of any BM programme is to observe and record the target behaviour(s) to obtain a baseline. In externally controlled BM programmes it is assumed that the presence of an independent neutral observer does not influence the nature or occurrence of the behaviour observed and recorded. However there are numerous studies which report that self-recording can be, and often is, a reactive process – the very act of recording one's own behaviour can function to effect change in the frequency of occurrence of the behaviour self-recorded.

## THE REACTIVITY OF SELF-RECORDING

There are a number of different possible explanations that can account for the reactivity of self-recording.

### *Operant explanation*

This is based on the 'law' that behaviour is highly influenced by its consequences. Therefore when a pupil records a positive behavioural occurrence, e.g. arrived at a lesson on time, refrained from losing his or her temper, the act of recording the positive, desirable behaviour functions as a positive consequence (reinforcement): therefore the probability that the same behaviour(s) will recur in the future is increased. This explanation of the reactivity of self-recording has an important corollary: the self-recording of negative aspects of one's own behaviour, e.g. arriving late at a lesson, fighting, losing one's temper, can function as an aversive (punishing) consequence. If possible, aversive consequences are avoided: the pupil may therefore avoid the aversive consequences by refraining from engaging in the inappropriate behaviours; but it is also possible that the pupil will avoid the aversive consequence/feedback by discontinuing the self-monitoring.

Therefore it is crucial that, wherever possible, pupils are asked to self-monitor positive aspects of their own behaviour as this maximises the chances of harnessing the reactivity of self-recording.

### *Self-regulation model explanation*

The self-monitoring of one's own behaviour is akin to creating self produced feedback. In any area of activity a pupil may aim to behave in certain ways, i.e. set standards or goals. The self-monitoring data therefore facilitates in a more conscious, precise manner the process of self-evaluation. The self produced feedback may provide data that confirms the pupil in their current behaviour because it agrees with or is congruent with his/her standards. If the self produced feedback provides data that are incongruent with the pupil's standards then this 'new' information may motivate the pupil to change his or her behaviour in ways which will help the behaviour to approximate more closely to the self set standard. The self-regulation model provides a rationale for all three possible outcomes of self-monitoring:

(i)    the pupil *does not* self-monitor.
(ii)   the pupil self-monitors but there is *no reactivity,* i.e. no behaviour change;
(iii)  the pupil self-monitors and *reactivity* (behaviour change) occurs.

Where the *pupil does not self-monitor* the pupil may have made no commitment to change his or her behaviour or was coerced into making a commitment to change, and therefore does not comply with the task demand of self-recording. In instances where the *pupil self-monitors but no reactivity occurs,* there are three explanations of this outcome:

(i)    The pupil had no commitment to change but self-monitored because of external pressures.
(ii)   The pupil was committed to change but had set no internal standard or a very vague internal standard, e.g. 'to try and do better', and so the process of self-evaluation was difficult or impossible to carry out.
(iii)  The pupil lacked the skills necessary to bridge the gap between commitment to the self-change programme and execution of the programme. An example of this would be a pupil whose problem behaviour was losing his or her temper. The pupil may have expressed genuine commitment to control their temper and proceeded to record all occasions 'when I felt I was going to lose my temper but didn't', i.e. the positive alternative.

In such a situation lack of a successful outcome should not be interpreted as indicating that the self-monitoring intervention was redundant, for it can serve two assessment functions. First, it can establish that the pupil's commitment to change was genuine and second, it can indicate the need to help the pupil acquire temper control strategies. In addition to these two *assessment functions* the self-recording *engaged the pupil* in the programme and thus provided the supervising teacher with an opportunity to reinforce the pupil for programme engagement.

While self-recording positive behaviours enhances the probability that the reactivity of self-recording will be harnessed nonetheless, sometimes the negative, unwanted problematic behaviour is recorded to aid problem analysis and the choice of the most appropriate intervention programme. Thus in the case of 'losing temper' the pupil may be asked to keep a diary of the occasions when they lost their temper, the build up to losing their temper (the antecedents) and the outcome (consequences). Such information is helpful to the functional analysis which in turn will aid the identification of the most appropriate temper control strategies for the pupil to acquire. The second intervention programme may then involve the pupil self-monitoring the occasions when the temper control strategies were successfully applied (the main emphasis) and less than successfully applied – emphasised less but necessary for further functional analysis.

# GUIDELINES FOR COMMITMENT TO A SELF-MONITORING PROGRAMME

(i)  *Commitment is easier* if the programme onset is delayed, and harder if the programme onset is immediate. An immediate behavioural homework, if set, can function both as an assessment of degree of commitment and as part of the actual self-management programme. If pupil commitment to a change programme has been 'hard won' then it may be appropriate to set an 'easy' behavioural homework to consolidate the pupil's commitment to change and to create opportunities to reinforce programme engagement. For example, if the major problem of concern was verbal abuse by the pupil towards the teacher and a very minor concern was the pupil's very occasional late arrival at school, then the latter problem might first be addressed by self-monitoring. Why? Because the probability of the pupil self-recording positive aspects of their behaviour (arriving on time) is high and thus 'success' for the pupil to positively self-evaluate and self-reinforce is almost guaranteed: such a positive experience will facilitate positive reinforcement from the teacher both for programme compliance and programme success. Such a positive experience will help to sustain pupil engagement when the more problematic behaviour becomes the focus of the self-management programme.

(ii)  *Commitment is easier* if the pupil has experienced a history of receiving positive reinforcement for promise-making and harder if past failure to keep promises was punished. Thus failure to keep promises should not be responded to by punishment but should be received as feedback indicating that a reassessment of pupil commitment, pupil skill repertoire, programme content and programme teacher support are all indicated.

(iii)  *Commitment is easier* if the behaviour to be changed is private and cannot easily be checked and harder if the intended behaviour change is publicly observable. It is nonetheless crucial that the behaviour to be changed is publicly observable. An example of an 'easy' commitment is 'try harder' – for it is private, unverifiable and not amenable to differential measurement. In contrast 'arrive at first lesson before 9.05 a.m.' is a more operationally useful commitment in that it is easily monitored by both the pupil and significant others. It is perhaps a more difficult commitment to make – for the behaviour is public, verifiable and amenable to differential measurement, i.e. the degree to which the pupil may fall short of the standard can be monitored (arrived at 9.07 a.m., 9.21 a.m. and so on).

(iv)  *Commitment is harder* if the problematic behaviour is not perceived to be under the pupil's own control, 'It's the teachers fault'. Counselling should aim to encourage a perception of an internal locus of control.

(v)  *Commitment is harder* if the pupil does not anticipate support for programme planning and execution.

(vi)  *Commitment is harder* if the pupil perceives the consequences of non-fulfilment of programme demands as excessively punitive.

## GUIDELINES FOR SUCCESSFUL SELF-MONITORING

For successful self-monitoring to occur it is necessary to elicit pupil compliance, i.e. it is necessary for the pupil to carry out the assignment in the manner agreed with the teacher. Therefore before self-monitoring is initiated it is necessary to assess if obstacles to compliance exist. The three main obstacles to pupil compliance are:

(i)     Lack of skills and/or knowledge necessary to complete some or all of the task assignments.

(ii)    The pupil's opinions about

- his or her 'problem' situation
- the ability of the teacher to offer effective help
- the value/usefulness of the assignment
- the pupil's experience of success/lack of success of previous 'help'
- the nature of the help offered – the pupil may expect to play a passive role while the teacher/counsellor tackles the pupil's problem(s)
- the effort involved in completing the assignment.

(iii)   The pupil's environment elicits non-compliance.

*Effective self-monitoring* is facilitated by:

(i)     *Specificity of task demand*: for example

- 'work harder' is not specific
- 'complete all classwork and homework' is specific
- 'behave in a more mature manner' is not specific
- 'do not giggle in lessons', 'raise your hand for teacher attention' are specific.

(ii)    *Giving skill training* if necessary, e.g. if 'losing temper' is the problem, practise temper control strategies via role play, mental rehearsal.

(iii)   *Self-monitoring positive behaviour* whenever possible: for example

- self-monitor 'arrived on time' not 'arrived late'
- 'handed in homework' not 'did not hand in homework'
- 'exercised temper control' not 'lost temper'
- 'cooperated well' not 'argued with peers'.

Nonetheless it is sometimes necessary to self-monitor details of problem behaviours to either aid functional analysis or evaluate the effect of intervention.

(iv)    *Reinforcing (encourage) compliance*

- encourage self-monitoring – for the pupil has then engaged in the self-management programme
- encourage accurate self-monitoring – for this is an indication of the value the pupil places on the assignment
- encourage reactivity, i.e. behaviour change.

It is sometimes necessary to 'shape up' the pupil's self-monitoring behaviour from inaccurate and perhaps careless, through accurate self-monitoring to reactive self-monitoring. The recording of data by the pupil provides the teacher with problem/non problem data which can provide the focus for problem orientated pupil counselling.

(v) *Starting with small 'easy' assignments* and gradually increase the assignments in terms of demands and relevance.

(vi) *Cues or reminders to self-monitor* should be structured into the programme: for example

- agree that the self-monitoring card/booklet should be kept in view on the desk
- agree that the self-monitoring card/booklet should be completed when the bell sounds at the end of the lesson
- agree that the subject teacher(s) should remind the pupil to self-monitor at the end of the lesson (this cue is more appropriate when conjoint monitoring (pupil and teacher) is practised.

The more frequent the conjoint pupil/teacher reviews the greater will be the degree of pupil compliance, as the meetings act as cues as well as providing opportunities for the teacher to provide and the pupil receive positive reinforcement for programme compliance and/or behaviour change.

(vii) *A personal, i.e. self-motivated, commitment* should be elicited from the pupil: this will enhance the probability of the pupil self-monitoring without undue reliance on external cues.

(viii) *A public commitment* to change should be elicited from the pupil: this both enhances the probability of significant others cueing the pupil to continue programme engagement and eliciting positive responses from significant others to reinforce programme compliance and/or behaviour change.

(ix) *Cognitive rehearsal strategies* – somewhat advanced techniques – can also enhance programme compliance. Two strategies of this nature are

(a) visual motor behaviour rehearsal
(b) self-instructional training.

*Visual motor behaviour rehearsal.* Using this method (used extensively in the field of sports psychology) the pupil is encouraged to relax, and visualise the successful behaviour – e.g. anger control, completing the self-monitoring assignment.

*Self-instructional training.* This approach involves

- preparing for the stressor, i.e. anticipating the problems, and working out appropriate responses (deep breathing, counting to ten, imagining relaxing scenes)
- confronting the stressor, i.e. activating the coping strategies rehearsed earlier
- using subvocal reinforcing self-statements on successful completion of assignments.

The teacher should try to anticipate and *reduce the possible negative side effects* of self-monitoring. This is pursued by the teacher exploring with the pupil possible negative consequences of successful self-monitoring, e.g. peer group disapproval, lack of teacher appreciation of pupil effort. A useful strategy to counter possible negative effects of self-monitoring is stress inoculation, i.e. encouraging the pupil to anticipate and imagine experiencing the negative side effects but then to proceed and imagine the successful completion of the assignment.

If possible, *independent verification* of the accuracy of self-monitoring should be obtained, e.g. consult subject teachers.

## EXAMPLES OF PUPIL SELF-MANAGEMENT PROTOCOLS

The self-monitoring booklets provided for pupils who articulate an intention to change their behaviour should be attractive, for this communicates to the pupil that the activity they are engaged in is of importance. The attractiveness of the booklets is enhanced if they have the appearance of a 'professional' production. This can be achieved by using good quality materials, and desk top publishing technology.

Reproduced below are constituent parts of a self-monitoring booklet, with accompanying comments.

### The Self-Monitoring Diary

The diary should be attractive in appearance and small enough to fit easily into a blazer or shirt pocket. A plastic wallet helps prevent the diary becoming grubby.

- Ownership of the diary – and by implication responsibility for the behaviour change programme – is firmly with the pupil (see Figure 5.3).
- The personal nature of the commitment and endeavour is emphasised by the 'private and confidential' notation (see Figure 5.4).
- The personal nature of the commitment is further emphasised by the 'I' pronoun (see Figure 5.5).
- The general goal of 'improved behaviour' is broken down into specific targets (Figure 5.5).
- The specific targets are couched in positive terms (Figure 5.5).
- A range of self-assessments for each behaviour (rated 1 to 5) is available.
- The pupil is invited to identify
  - a short-term goal (lesson target)
  - a medium-term goal (daily target)
  - a long-term goal (weekly target). (See Figure 5.6.)
- The pupil's signed commitment is witnessed by the member of staff monitoring the programme. Thus the commitment is 'public', which enhances the probability of programme compliance.
- The pupil reaffirms his or her commitment to improve their behaviour at the beginning of each school day (see Figure 5.7).
- In addition the pupil specifies/describes the specific target behaviours and personalises the commitment by signing the Statement of Intent daily.
- Public evaluation (see Figure 5.8) of achieved lesson, daily and weekly total with targets (see page 3 of Diary, Figure 5.6) facilitates positive self-evaluation and harnesses the reinforcement property of goal achievement which as a side effect also reinforces commitment to the programme.
- Goal achievement often results in the pupil setting higher goals in the future.
- When reviewing the programme with the pupil one should be alert to identify opportunities to facilitate and encourage realistic but 'higher' targets.
- The various combinations of scores, e.g. by lesson, by day, by week, a.m., p.m., by subject, can be processed and graphed. The data, processed and

presented in this way, can provide positive feedback to reinforce pupil engagement in the programme, behaviour change and 'higher' target setting.

- The data can be processed in many different ways. The principles that dictate data processing and feedback are: identify and feed back data indicative of successful change – or at least change in the desired direction; and identify data that can be used to promote positive restructuring (see page 84). For example, if 'geography is the worst lesson' is the pupil's perception, then abstract out and feed back data which indicates the contrary: if the pupil's perception is 'Mondays are awful', then abstract out and feed back data which indicates Mondays are 'getting better'. On occasions creativity has to be exercised to identify and abstract out data of this nature.

It is important to maximise the number of comparisons made by the pupil so that positive achievements can be identified, recognised and reinforced. Such positive self-evaluations reinforce programme compliance and enhance the possibility of the pupil being further motivated to set themselves even higher standards to strive towards.

**Figure 5.3** A Self-Monitoring Diary

# Self
# Monitoring Diary

This is the personal property of

*Alan Smith*

......................................................

PRIVATE AND CONFIDENTIAL

**Figure 5.4** A Self-Monitoring Diary, page 1

## Statement of Intent

I am going to try and improve my behaviour.
To do this I will:

    i) ....*complete set work*..................

    ii) ....*stay in my seat*....................

    iii) ....*not disturb others*...............

I will rate my behaviour as follows:-

    very good ........................5

    good ..............................4

    satisfactory ......................3

    poor ..............................2

    very poor ........................1

                  *A. Smith*
Signed ..................................................

– 2 –

**Figure 5.5** A Self-Monitoring Diary, page 2

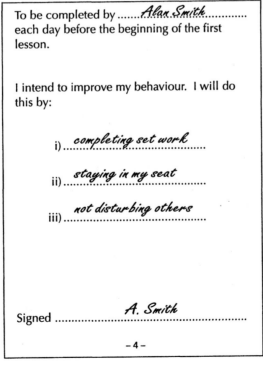

**Goals**

I am aiming to achieve at least
........9........ marks in each **lesson.**

I am aiming to achieve at least
........63........ marks every **day.**

I am aiming to achieve at least
........315........ marks this **week.**

Signed................A. Smith................Pupil

Signed ................H O'Year................Witness

– 3 –

**Figure 5.6** A Self-Monitoring Diary, page 3

To be completed by .......Alan Smith..............
each day before the beginning of the first
lesson.

I intend to improve my behaviour. I will do
this by:

i) ........completing set work........

ii) ........staying in my seat........

iii) ........not disturbing others........

Signed ................A. Smith................

– 4 –

**Figure 5.7** A Self-Monitoring Diary, page 4 (repeated as pages 6, 8, 10 and 12)

| Date 7/3/94 | BEHAVIOUR | | | |
| --- | --- | --- | --- | --- |
| Lesson | (i) *working* | (ii) *in seat* | (iii) *not disturbing others* | Total |
| 1 *Geog.* | 3 | 5 | 5 | 13 |
| 2 *Maths* | 4 | 4 | 5 | 13 |
| 3 *History* | 3 | 4 | 2 | 9 |
| 4 *C.D.T.* | 5 | 5 | 5 | 15 |
| 5 *French* | 2 | 3 | 2 | 7 |
| 6 *R.E.* | 1 | 3 | 2 | 6 |
| 7 *English* | 3 | 4 | 3 | 10 |
| TOTAL | 21 | 28 | 24 | 73 |

– 5 –

**Weekly Review**

1. Lesson Target – My lesson target was....*9*.... Out of...*35*..lessons I achieved this lesson target..*25*..times.

2. Daily Target – My daily target was...*63*... Out of....*5*....days I achieved this daily target on....*5*....days.

3. Weekly Target – My target for the week was..*315*.... I did / ~~did not~~ achieve my target.

Target..*315*..          Difference
Actual..*375*..              +60

–14 –

**Figure 5.8** A Self-Monitoring Diary, page 5 (repeated as pages 7, 9, 11 and 13)

**Figure 5.9** A Self-Monitoring Diary, page 14

## POSITIVE RESTRUCTURING

The process of *positive restructuring is an essential component of the reviewing process.* Negative feedback can be aversive to pupils: this aversive consequence can be avoided by opting out of the behaviour change programme. Therefore to keep the pupil engaged in the programme all feedback should be couched in positive terms whenever possible. Examples of positive feedback are:

(a) Four late arrivals would be restructured 'you were early six times last week'.
(b) Being sent out of one lesson for misbehaviour would be restructured 'you completed 34 lessons last week'.
(c) Falling short of the lesson target in three lessons might be restrudured in a number of ways
  – 'You achieved your lesson target 32 times last week'.
  – 'You achieved your lesson target in every lesson on four days last week'.
  – 'You achieved your lesson target every morning last week and on two afternoons'.

The purpose of positive restructuring is to:

(a) emphasise and reinforce positive achievement;
(b) aid consolidation of positive behaviour change by recognition and reinforment;
(c) aiding explicit and realistic target setting for the next phase of the programme.

**Teacher's Observations**

*A good week's effort, John.*

*You reached your weekly target and daily targets, great!*

*Success in reaching your R.E. and French targets will help you achieve your lesson target in all lessons.*

*Have you decided on next week's targets yet?*

*H. O'Year*

– 15 –

**Figure 5.10** Self-Monitoring Diary, page 15

Figure 5.10 illustrates page 15 of the Diary. This shows that:

(a) John's efforts and achievements are recognised in a friendly, positive and personal way.
(b) Positive restructuring is modelled for the pupil – to promote the pupil dwelling on positive achievements.
(c) John is cued to consider the 'new' targets consequent to dwelling on recent achievements – this increases the likelihood of John setting 'higher' targets and striving to 'beat' the previous week's achievements.

The review of the previous week's achievements resulted in John setting two targets both of which represent 'improvements' on the previous week (Figure 5.11). Again there is a personal signed commitment and a witness – so that the commitment is not private and covert but public and overt.

The example of a Self-Monitoring Diary illustrated in this chapter is but one of many that can be produced to facilitate pupil self-management programmes. For example, different phrases and local expressions may add to the face validity of the programme. In addition, the appeal of the booklet can be maximised by using phraseology and concepts with which the pupils have a particular affinity.

## Variations of the Self-Monitoring Diary

*Variation 1.* Pages 2 and 3 can be collapsed into one page as illustrated in Figure 5.12.

*Variation 2.* Page 2 can be couched in specific goal theory terms as illustrated in Figure 5.13.

**Forward Planning**

Next week *I aim to:*

1. *reach my targets in all my lessons.*

2. *increase my weekly target to 375 points.*

signed.............*A. Smith*...........................

witness ............*H. O''Year*.......................

– 16 –

**Figure 5.11** Self-Monitoring Diary, page 16

**Statement of Intent**

I am going to try and improve my behaviour.
To do this I will:

i) ............*complete set work*.............

ii) ............*not disturb others*............

iii) ............‾............................

> ***Rating Scale:*** very poor (5); poor (4);
> satisfactory (3): good (4); very good (5)

I am going to achieve:-

i) ............*8 points every lesson*.........

ii) ............*56 points every day*...........

iii) ............*280 points this week*..........

Signed...........................................

Witness ...........................................

– 2 –

**Figure 5.12** Variation 1

```
┌─────────────────────────────────────┐
│            ┌──────────┐              │
│            │   Goal   │              │
│            └──────────┘              │
│  I am going to try very hard to improve my  │
│  behaviour in all my lessons.        │
│                                      │
│  TARGETS                             │
│  To achieve my goal I will concentrate my   │
│  efforts on the following:           │
│                                      │
│  Target 1. ...not shout out...       │
│                                      │
│  Target 2. ...stay in my seat...     │
│                                      │
│  Target 3. ...not disturb others...  │
│                                      │
│                                      │
│  Signed...A. Smith...                │
│                                      │
│  Witness ...H. O'Year...             │
│                                      │
│               – 3 –                  │
└─────────────────────────────────────┘
```

**Figure 5.13** Variation 2

*Variation 3.* Page 3 can be very functional in terms of the semantics, and simple (a dichotomous rating) in terms of recording, as illustrated in Figure 5.14.

*Variation 4.* Page 5 – the monitoring protocol – should be presented as attractively as possible and laid out so that the data is easily assessed, i.e. on inspecting the data a person should not have to ask 'What does this mean?'

If the self assessment is dichotomous, i.e. 'Yes, I did' or 'No, I did not', then page 5 could take a number of forms. Two such forms are illustrated in Figures 5.15 and 5.16.

The premise on which this self-monitoring practice is based is that the pupil wants to improve his or her behaviour: the teacher's role is that of facilitator. However a number of outcomes can result from the exercise.

(i)   The pupil fails to self-monitor: in this case it may be suggested to the pupil that conjoint teacher–pupil monitoring will help him or her to realise the commitment to self-monitor (see next section).

(ii)  The pupil self-monitors but no behaviour change ensues: in this case address the following questions.

(a) Has the pupil the *academic skills* to achieve the target behaviour?
(b) Has the pupil the *social skills* to achieve the target behaviour?
(c) Does the pupil *know how* to apply the above skills?
(d) Does the pupil *know when* to apply the above skills?
(e) Does the pupil know when he or she has successfully applied the above skills (i.e. do they receive feedback)?
(f) Does the pupil have the necessary *directions and instructions* to follow?

---

**Statement of Intent**

I am going to check my own behaviour.

I will put a tick in the appropriate box if :

Target 1. *arrived at the lesson on time*

Target 2. *brought all equipment*

Target 3. *paid attention during the lesson*

Target 4. *did not disturb other pupils*

Signed *A. Smith*

Witness *H. O'Year*

– 2 –

---

**Figure 5.14** Variation 3

| Date *4th Apr.* Lesson | GOALS | Goal Achieved | | Pupil's Initials |
|---|---|---|---|---|
| 1 *French* | 1. Arrived on time<br>2. Worked quietly<br>3. No shouting | YES<br>YES<br>YES | NO<br>NO<br>NO | *AS* |
| 2 *English* | 1. Arrived on time<br>2. Worked quietly<br>3. No shouting | YES<br>YES<br>YES | NO<br>NO<br>NO | *AS* |
| 3 *R.E.* | 1. Arrived on time<br>2. Worked quietly<br>3. No shouting | YES<br>YES<br>YES | NO<br>NO<br>NO | *AS* |
| 4 *Games* | 1. Arrived on time<br>2. Worked quietly<br>3. No shouting | YES<br>YES<br>YES | NO<br>NO<br>NO | *AS* |
| 5 *C.D.T.* | 1. Arrived on time<br>2. Worked quietly<br>3. No shouting | YES<br>YES<br>YES | NO<br>NO<br>NO | *AS* |
| 6 *History* | 1. Arrived on time<br>2. Worked quietly<br>3. No shouting | YES<br>YES<br>YES | NO<br>NO<br>NO | *AS* |
| 7 *Geog.* | 1. Arrived on time<br>2. Worked quietly<br>3. No shouting | YES<br>YES<br>YES | NO<br>NO<br>NO | *AS* |

**Figure 5.15** Variation 4

If a negative answer is obtained for one or more of the above questions then the question needs to be addressed in its own right. If the answers to the above questions are all affirmative then pupil or instructional deficits can be ruled out as

| Date *1/4/94* | GOALS | | | | Total |
|---|---|---|---|---|---|
| Lesson | *arrive on time* | *have equipment* | *complete work* | *follow rules* | |
| 1 *Germ.* | ✓ | ✓ | ✓ | ✓ | *4* |
| 2 *Geog.* | ✓ | ✓ | ✓ | ✓ | *4* |
| 3 *P.E.* | ✓ | ✓ | ✓ | ✓ | *4* |
| 4 *History* | ✗ | ✓ | ✓ | ✓ | *3* |
| 5 *Maths* | ✓ | ✓ | ✓ | ✓ | *4* |
| 6 *Science* | ✓ | ✓ | ✓ | ✓ | *4* |
| 7 *French* | ✗ | ✓ | ✗ | ✓ | *2* |
| TOTAL | *5* | *7* | *6* | *7* | *25* |

**Figure 5.16** Variation 5

contributory factors to the lack of change in pupil behaviour. In this case a number of further questions can be asked. These are:

(g) Does the change in behaviour result in a *gain for the pupil* (e.g. reward, relief, praise, competence, self-esteem)?

(h) Does the change in behaviour result in a *loss for the pupil* (e.g. punishment, ridicule, failure, peer group alienation)?

(i) Does the change in behaviour have a *neutral outcome?*

If the environment is not supportive of the behaviour change aimed for then the task of behaviour change for the pupil is harder. Positive environmental consequences should be structured whenever possible to support the pupil self-change behaviour programme, e.g. prompt subject teachers to give merit awards, comment favourably on behaviour when marking classwork. If the environment is not supportive of the behaviour change and this is anticipated, this should be made known to the pupil in as explicit terms as possible. This procedure, known as 'stress inoculation', will enhance the probability of the pupil remaining engaged in the behaviour change programme when aversive environmental consequences result – it is an attempt to inoculate the pupil against failure.

## CONJOINT PUPIL–TEACHER MONITORING

The on-report system is recommended when there is little, if any, pupil commitment to change. Consequently it is substantially teacher determined and conforms to the *administrative model* of change, i.e. the pupil is substantially passive.

The pupil self-management practices described above conform to the *participative model* of change, i.e. the pupil is active. The various practices recommended when there is substantial pupil commitment are determined as far as possible by the pupil. It is sometimes the case that there is some pupil commitment to change – but perhaps not enough for it to be judged sufficient to introduce a self-management programme, yet sufficient to reject an on-report practice as inappropriate. In such cases a conjoint pupil–teacher self-monitoring programme could be utilised. Such a practice has the following advantages:

(i)   External validation of the accuracy of pupil self-monitoring is provided.

(ii)  Discrepancies between pupil self-rating and teacher ratings provides data for problem orientated counselling.

(iii) It can be used to elicit encouragement and support (reinforcement) from the teachers engaged in the conjoint monitoring and thus:

– consolidate the pupil's engagement in the programme and commitment to the behaviour change programme, and
– reinforce behaviour change.

The 'software' for conjoint monitoring is very similar to both the on-report protocols and pupit self-management protocols, but it is drafted to accommodate both teacher assessment and pupil self-assessment.

### Examples of conjoint pupil–teacher monitoring protocols

The presentation requirements are the same as for the self-monitoring diaries or booklets – namely, attractive appearance, convenient size and relevant content.

The title of the booklet (Figure 5.17) reflects the fact that the pupil and teachers are cooperating on a joint endeavour: the pupil's role is to effect change in

**Figure 5.17** Cooperative Monitoring Diary (example 1)

```
┌─────────────────────────────────────────────┐
│   ┌─────────────────────────────────────┐   │
│   │                                     │   │
│   │         Co-operative                │   │
│   │       Monitoring Diary              │   │
│   │                                     │   │
│   │                                     │   │
│   │    This is the personal property of │   │
│   │                                     │   │
│   │    .....Andrew Goodit.....          │   │
│   │                                     │   │
│   │                                     │   │
│   │    PRIVATE AND CONFIDENTIAL         │   │
│   │                                     │   │
│   └─────────────────────────────────────┘   │
│                   – 1 –                       │
└─────────────────────────────────────────────┘
```

**Figure 5.18** Cooperative Monitoring Diary, page 1

```
┌─────────────────────────────────────────────┐
│                                               │
│               YOUR GOAL                       │
│                                               │
│   Name:.......Andrew Goodit.......during the next │
│   ....2....weeks you should try to .....follow the ..... │
│   .....teacher's instructions and work hard..... │
│                                               │
│              YOUR TARGETS                     │
│   I will know you are working on this goal whenever I see you: │
│       (a) .....complete class work.....       │
│       (b) .....working quietly.....           │
│       (c) .....not interfering with others..... │
│                                               │
│              GOOD LUCK !                       │
│                  – 2 –                         │
└─────────────────────────────────────────────┘
```

**Figure 5.19** Cooperative Monitoring Diary, page 2

personal behaviour and the role of the teachers is to facilitate the change by providing feedback on a lesson by lesson basis. This regularity of feedback provides frequent opportunities for the teachers to positively reinforce desired changes in pupil behaviour.

Ownership of the Monitoring Diary is given to the pupil (Figure 5.18). This is an 'encouragement' for the pupil to also accept 'ownership' of his or her behaviour. The pupil's commitment is spelt out in explicit terms, by the pupil (Figure 5.20) but this is preceded by the supervising teacher clearly describing the pupil's goal by identifying up to three specific behaviours (Figure 5.19). The 'Good Luck'! salute is a friendly and supportive message from the teacher which communicates a facilative disposition and not a punitive one.

---

**MY GOAL**

My Name is: ...................*Andrew Goodit*...................I will try to

.................*improve my work and behaviour*.................

.........................................................................

**MY TARGETS**

You will know I am working on this goal whenever you see me:

(a) ...*doing my class work*...................

(b) ...*not talking or shouting out*...................

(c) ...*not messing about*...................

– 3 –

---

**Figure 5.20** Cooperative Monitoring Diary, page 3

---

**INSTRUCTIONS**

Pupil, Please

1.  Show this Diary to the teacher BEFORE the start of each lesson,

2.  Keep the Diary on your desk DURING the lesson,

3.  Ask the teacher to mark each target at the END of the lesson.

Teacher, Please

1.  Mark each target at the end of the lesson,

2.  Be supportive of effort and achievement,

3.  Make arrangements with the pupil to discuss discrepancies in marks.

| O  =  Unsatisfactory | I  =  Satisfactory |
|---|---|

– 4 –

---

**Figure 5.21** Cooperative Monitoring Diary, page 4

The Diary is shown to the teacher at the beginning of the lesson: consequently the teacher is made aware at the beginning of the lesson that a particular pupil's behaviour has to be rated at the end of the lesson (Figure 5.21).

The Diary is kept in sight on the pupil's desk during the lesson: consequently the pupil has a constant visual reminder on the desk that the teacher will assess his or her behaviour during the lesson and rate it at the end of the lesson. This 'visual reminder' might cue the pupil to self-monitor and self-evaluate their behaviour during the course of the lesson.

At the end of the lesson the pupil self assesses their behaviour with respect to the three target behaviours. This provides an opportunity for

| Date 21/3/94 | GOALS | | | | | | Total | Teacher's Initials |
|---|---|---|---|---|---|---|---|---|
| Lesson | *class work* | | *working quietly* | | *no messing* | | | |
| | Teacher | Pupil | Teacher | Pupil | Teacher | Pupil | | |
| ¹ *R.E.* | 1 | 1 | 1 | 1 | 1 | 1 | 3/3 | FJ |
| ² *Geog.* | 1 | 1 | 0 | 1 | 1 | 1 | 2/3 | MC |
| ³ *Maths.* | 1 | 1 | 1 | 1 | 1 | 1 | 3/3 | NP |
| ⁴ *English* | 0 | 0 | 0 | 1 | 0 | 1 | 1/3 | SM |
| ⁵ *French* | 0 | 0 | 0 | 0 | 0 | 0 | 0/0 | JB |
| ⁶ *C.D.T.* | 1 | 1 | 1 | 1 | 1 | 1 | 3/3 | PB |
| ⁷ *History* | 1 | 1 | 0 | 1 | 1 | 1 | 2/3 | JH |
| | To Teacher: Please give 1 point or 0 point for each behaviour | | | | | | | |
| | To Pupil: Please give 1 point or 0 point for each behavour | | | | | | | |

– 5 –

**Figure 5.22** Cooperative Monitoring Diary, page 5 (repeated as pages 6, 7, 8 and 9)

positive self-evaluation and self-reinforcement. If the pupil is motivated to improve their behaviour then this positive self-evaluation and self-reinforcement may be sufficient to maintain and consolidate the 'improved' behaviour. However this may not be the case: if this had been a likely outcome the pupil would probably have been engaged in a self-management, not conjoint management programme.

The 'improved' behaviour can be maintained in a number of ways.

(i)   By *teacher recognition* of the improved behaviour, e.g. by statements such as 'Your behaviour has improved' and 'It's certainly showing in better work. . .keep it up!'

(ii)  By *setting goals,* which facilitates the processes of self-evaluation and self-reinforcement.

(iii) By linking the total scores achieved to privileges in a *behavioural contract.*

The layout of the page 5 (Figure 5.22) allows an easy assessment to be made of:

(i)   *overall behaviour in each lesson* (by scanning across the appropriate line;

(ii)  *each target behaviour* (by scanning down the appropriate column);

(iii) *overall behaviour during the course of the day* (by scrutinising the page);

(iv)  *agreement or otherwise of pupil self-assessment* with teacher assessment.

Page 10 of the Diary (Figure 5.23) facilitates the 'drawing together' of the record of the pupil's performance over the course of a week. The data can therefore be used to:

(i)   Provide *reinforcing feedback* to the pupil.

(ii)  Facilitate *positive restructuring* by reviewing the data with the pupil and making appropriate observations; for example

    – 'Look, three out of three in French . . . and you said Mr Hurley never gave you good marks!'

```
┌─────────────────────────────────────────────────────────────┐
│                     PUPIL REVIEW                            │
│                                                             │
│  Targets                                                    │
│                                                             │
│  1.    3 points in each lesson: Achieved in..24..out of..35..lessons │
│                                                             │
│  2.    21 points each day:     Achieved on...3....out of....5....days │
│                                                             │
│  3.    105 points each week:   This week I achieved...93...points │
│  Next Week .....I will try harder in English and French.......... │
│                                                             │
│  ........................................................... │
│                                                             │
│  Strategy ......1. Sit at the front......................... │
│                                                             │
│  .......2. Don't sit with John Alk......................... │
│                                                             │
│                          – 10 –                             │
└─────────────────────────────────────────────────────────────┘
```

**Figure 5.23** Cooperative Monitoring Diary, page 10

– 'Look, three out of three in all five maths lessons, and you said that was the lesson in which your behaviour was the worst!'
– 'Marvellous, you never lost a point for calling out in lessons – that's not your worst behaviour now!'

The intent of the positive restructuring is to facilitate a change in the pupil's self-image with respect to behaviour. We wish to promote a self-image of a pupil who can and does behave appropriately – for there is a tendency for people's actual behaviour to be consistent with their self-image.

The use of a conjoint teacher–pupil monitoring diary is indicative of a judgement that pupil self-motivation to change behaviour is insufficient to sustain a more pupil orientated intervention, i.e. the use of a pupil self-management protocol was contra-indicated. Therefore pupil behaviour change, when achieved, may not be maintained purely by pupil positive self-evaluation and self-reinforcement: external reinforcement of behaviour change will probably be required. This can be provided by linking the teacher rating of pupil behaviour to a behavioural contract. However such an intrusive intervention may not be required. Social reinforcement, i.e. teacher recognition and praise, may be sufficient and if so is preferable to a more intrusive intervention as it is 'more natural', i.e. does, or at least should, occur in the pupil's natural environment.

Positive teacher comments about desirable changes in pupil behaviour can be recorded on page 11 (Figure 5.24). The advantages of written positive reinforcement can then be harnessed, i.e. they have the potential to have a positive reinforcing effect each time it is read by the pupil.

As with most in-school pupil management programmes the effectiveness of the intervention can be enhanced by including a parental dimension. Daily, recorded parental involvement can be facilitated by the protocol illustrated on page 12 of the booklet (Figure 5.25).

**TEACHER REVIEW**

*Overall a much better week, well done.*

*You're right to concentrate on French and*

*English. Come and see me at 3.30 pm on Monday*

*as I'm keen to see how you get on in your first*

*French and English lessons of the week.*

*H. O'Year*

– 11 –

**Figure 5.24** Cooperative Monitoring Diary, page 11

**PARENTAL REVIEW**

| Day | Comment | Signature |
|-----|---------|-----------|
| Monday | *A good day except for French* | *S. Goodit* |
| Tuesday | *Very pleased* | *S. Goodit* |
| Wednesday | *French lesson much better* | *S. Goodit* |
| Thursday | *Another good day* | *S. Goodit* |
| Friday | *Andrew is doing great!* | *S. Goodit* |

*This has been an excellent week for Andrew.*

*His mum and I are very pleased*

– 12 –

**Figure 5.25** Cooperative Monitoring Diary, page 12

It will often help to both facilitate and accelerate pupil behaviour change if the parents are prompted to record positive comments about appropriate behaviour change, for this can both harness the benefits of written positive reinforcement and also provide prompts for the supervising teacher to facilitate positive restructuring on the part of the pupil (and even the parents) when appropriate.

### Variations of the teacher–pupil Monitoring Diary

The decision to utilise a conjoint teacher–pupil monitoring protocol will have been arrived at after an assesssment and consideration of the pupil's motivation to change. The decision will have been contributed to by the judgement that the pupil's 'internal' motivation was insufficient to sustain commitment to a self-management programme. Therefore external motivation in the form of positive consequences will probably be required to sustain the behaviour change. While such positive consequences may be incorporated into a behavioural contract, e.g. free time, pocket money, teacher recognition and praise may be sufficient. Thus, in addition to daily teacher and pupil monitoring of target behaviours space can be incorporated for positive teacher comments (Figure 5.26).

When this page is included in the Monitoring Diary it is desirable that all the pupil's teachers are 'primed' to record positive comments when the pupil's behaviour is satisfactory or better. A teacher prompt to this effect can be included inside the front cover (see Figure 5.27).

| REGISTRATION ON TIME : | | | | ( ) am ☐ pm ☐ | | |
|---|---|---|---|---|---|---|
| **DAY:** | | | | T1 = | | |
| | | | | T2 = | | |
| **Date:** | **T1** | **T2** | **T3** | T3 = | | |
| **Lesson** | Own Tch. | Own Tch. | Own Tch. | COMMENT | | Tch. |
| 1 | | | | | | |
| 2 | | | | | | |
| 3 | | | | | | |
| 4 | | | | | | |
| 5 | | | | | | |
| 6 | | | | | | |
| 7 | | | | | | |
| TOTALS | | | | | | |
| PARENT'S SIGNATURE: | | | | | | |

**Figure 5.26** Cooperative Monitoring Diary (Variation 1)

## TO YOUR TEACHERS

Please enter your rating (✓ or ✗) in the appropriate column and sign.

## IMPORTANT

Please discuss your ratings with the pupil.

When targets are met please give praise.

Thank you

**Figure 5.27** Teacher prompt to reinforce appropriate behaviour

The page illustrated in Figure 5.26 also includes a cell to record punctuality. This may be included because poor time keeping is a pupil behaviour of concern. It may also be included when the behaviour is not a problem – for in this case it will ensure that the pupil gets off to a 'good' start to the self-monitoring in that he or she starts both the morning and afternoon sessions with a positive self-recording.

The dichotomous scoring procedure described in the conjoint teacher–pupil monitoring booklet is a poor discriminator of pupil behaviour. For example the category 'satisfactory' incorporates the range of judgements from 'barely satisfactory' to 'excellent'. This is an inefficient behaviour change rating scale for two reasons. Firstly, a pupil may be behaving exceptionally well and warrant an 'excellent' rating if it were possible. In the absence of such a rating the pupil's behaviour may 'deteriorate' to a just acceptable level, i.e. to a level just sufficient to achieve a 'satisfactory' rating. Secondly, a pupil's behaviour may be unsatisfactory but nonetheless the pupil may be trying to improve his or her behaviour: in fact the pupil's behaviour may 'improve' from 'very unsatisfactory' to 'unsatisfactory'. The rating scale of 'satisfactory/unsatisfactory' would be insensitive to this change and hence the encouragement provided by positive feedback for the pupil to continue his or her efforts would be lost: the pupil may therefore 'give up'. Consequently a rating scale which facilitates *discriminative feedback* is often superior to a dichotmous rating scale. Thus the booklet described above could be modified to incorporate a 5 point rating scale and specific goal setting. Page 3 could be transposed to page 2 and an alternative page 3 added as illustrated in Figure 5.28. This structure to the target setting

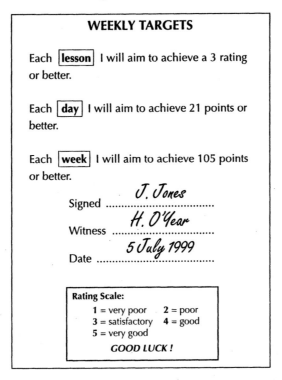

**Figure 5.28** Cooperative Monitoring Diary (Variation 2)

incorporates short-term goals (lesson by lesson), medium-term goals (day by day) and long-term goals (week by week).

It is important when using a 5 point scale that unrealistically high targets are not set. It should be established that satisfactory behaviour (rating 3) is perfectly acceptable. The achievement of realistic goals can be reinforcing to the pupil and may have the effect of leading the pupil to set higher targets in the following weeks. In contrast, initial failure to achieve unrealistically high targets can have a discouraging effect on pupils and lead to disaffection and 'giving up' behaviour.

The process of recording a pupil's rating in the booklet is important and the lack of time at the end of a lesson to interact with the pupil can sometimes weaken the effect of the conjoint monitoring as a behaviour change strategy. Therefore it can be helpful to the teachers to receive a 'reminder' to recognise improvements in behaviour. This reminder, together with a similar reminder to parents, could be included in the booklet on the page preceding the first day of conjoint monitoring as illustrated in Figure 5.29.

The illustrations of the on-report protocols presented in Chapter 3 are all amenable to development into conjoint teacher–pupil protocols by adding a pupil self-assessment column. The development of the 'Improved Behaviour Record' to encompass a pupil self-assessment dimension is illustrated in Figure 5.30.

Reference has been made on a number of occasions to the power of positive feedback in reinforcing both commitment to change and the achievement of change and its facilitative function in encouraging pupils to strive for 'harder' targets.

---

**To the Teacher**

In order to help Arthur improve his / her behaviour he / she has agreed to complete a joint monitoring diary.

Please score *Arthur's* behaviour in each target area from 1 to 5 and give praise when *Arthur's* behaviour is satisfactory or better.

If your ratings differ greatly from *Arthur's* ratings please arrange to see *Arthur* to discuss the differencies.

            Thank you for your cooperation

**To the Parents**

Please look at this booklet each night with your son / daughter. If you sign the page we will know that you have reviewed *Arthur's* day's behaviour with him / her.

Please be positive where satisfactory ratings have been achieved: if unsatisfactory ratings have been recorded please discuss them with *Arthur* and offer advice and guidance.

Please consult with *Mr. H. O'Year* at school if you are considering imposing a sanction – we do not want *Arthur* to be punished twice for the same misbehaviour.

            Thank you for your cooperation

---

**Figure 5.29** Cooperative Monitoring Diary (Variation 3)

**IMPROVED BEHAVIOUR RECORD**

| Lesson: ...................................... | 1 | | 2 | | 3 | | 4 | | 5 | | 6 | | 7 | |
|---|---|---|---|---|---|---|---|---|---|---|---|---|---|---|
| | T | P | T | P | T | P | T | P | T | P | T | P | T | P |
| 1. Arrived on time to the lesson | | | | | | | | | | | | | | |
| 2. Brought the right equipment | | | | | | | | | | | | | | |
| 3. Attentive during the lesson | | | | | | | | | | | | | | |
| 4. Not disturbing others | | | | | | | | | | | | | | |
| 5. Followed instructions | | | | | | | | | | | | | | |
| 6. Completed the classwork | | | | | | | | | | | | | | |
| 7. Polite and well mannered | | | | | | | | | | | | | | |
| 1. Late to lesson | | | | | | | | | | | | | | |
| 2. Inadequate or no equipment | | | | | | | | | | | | | | |
| 3. Inattentive during lesson | | | | | | | | | | | | | | |
| 4. Disturbed others | | | | | | | | | | | | | | |
| 5. Did not follow instructions | | | | | | | | | | | | | | |
| 6. Insufficient classwork | | | | | | | | | | | | | | |
| 7. Impolite and/or ill mannered | | | | | | | | | | | | | | |

**Form Teacher's comment and signature**



**Parent / Guardian comment and signature**

**Figure 5.30** Teacher–pupil monitoring: the 'Improved Behaviour Record'

Visual presentation of feedback data often enhances the power of positive feedback. This phenomenon can be harnessed in virtually all the monitoring systems described – be they teacher managed, pupil self-managed or conjointly managed by teacher and pupil. One example of such a protocol is illustrated in Figure 5.31. This is somewhat complicated and merely plotting 'scores achieved' on graph paper can be equally effective.

## CONCLUSION

The purpose of this Chapter has been to present practical pupil self-management practices to teachers in the Secondary sector. A parallel purpose has been to present the theoretical rationale which generates the practices.

When the theoretical rationale is understood, the manifestations of the theory in terms of the content and presentation of monitoring booklets is infinite – the limiting factor is the creativity of the teachers applying the theory in practical situations . . . and every teacher could perhaps create and add at least one further variant to the range that already exists.

# BEHAVIOUR BAROMETER CHART

Pupil ................................................................    Week beginning ...........................................

At the end of each lesson pupil fills in own grade assessment;  then the teacher fills in his / her assessment.

| PERIOD | | Mon. | Tues. | Wed. | Thurs. | Fri. | TOTAL |
|---|---|---|---|---|---|---|---|
| 1 | Pupil | | | | | | |
| 1 | Teacher | | | | | | |
| 2 | Pupil | | | | | | |
| 2 | Teacher | | | | | | |
| 3 | Pupil | | | | | | |
| 3 | Teacher | | | | | | |
| 4 | Pupil | | | | | | |
| 4 | Teacher | | | | | | |
| 5 | Pupil | | | | | | |
| 5 | Teacher | | | | | | |
| 6 | Pupil | | | | | | |
| 6 | Teacher | | | | | | |
| 7 | Pupil | | | | | | |
| 7 | Teacher | | | | | | |

| Mark | Rating |
|---|---|
| 1 | *Very Poor: Severely disruptive* |
| 2 | *Poor: Mild / Moderately disruptive* |
| 3 | *Satisfactory* |
| 4 | *Good:  Better than many members of the class* |
| 5 | *Very Good:  Better than most members of the class* |

| | |
|---|---|
| *Weekly Target* | |
| *Pupil's Weekly Total* | |
| *Teacher's Weekly Total* | |

## PERFORMANCE BAROMETER

| DAILY BAROMETER | | VERY POOR | POOR | SATISFACTORY | GOOD | VERY GOOD |
|---|---|---|---|---|---|---|
| | | 7 | 14 | 21 | 28 | 35 |
| Mon. | Pupil's Total | | | | | |
| Mon. | Teacher's Total | | | | | |
| Tues. | Pupil's Total | | | | | |
| Tues. | Teacher's Total | | | | | |
| Wed. | Pupil's Total | | | | | |
| Wed. | Teacher's Total | | | | | |
| Thurs. | Pupil's Total | | | | | |
| Thurs. | Teacher's Total | | | | | |
| Fri. | Pupil's Total | | | | | |
| Fri. | Teacher's Total | | | | | |

| WEEKLY BAROMETER | VERY POOR | POOR | SATISFACTORY | GOOD | VERY GOOD |
|---|---|---|---|---|---|
| | 35 | 70 | 105 | 140 | 175 |
| Pupil's Total | | | | | |
| Teacher's Total | | | | | |

**Figure 5.31** The Behaviour Barometer Chart

# CHAPTER 6

# Anxiety management: the troubled student

The aims of this chapter are to:

(i)     Describe anxiety.
(ii)    Identify when anxiety is a problem.
(iii)   Consider anxiety problems in childhood and adolescence.
(iv)    Describe the assessment and management of anxiety.
(v)     Present six case studies of anxiety management.

Pupils with mental health problems have received scant consideration compared with those pupils with conduct disorders – for the conduct disordered child is readily identified by teachers.

In contrast, teachers may be unaware of pupils who are experiencing mental health problems: yet such problems may in exceptional and thankfully rare cases lead to pupils attempting to take their own lives.

Anxiety is often associated with many different mental health problems. This chapter seeks to raise teacher awareness about this not uncommon mental health problem experienced by children and young people, namely anxiety. Such awareness will help teachers to fulfil their responsibilities to the emotional development of children – a responsibility spelt out in DfE Circular 8/94 in the following words:

> The emotional development of children must continue to be a concern of mainstream education. (DfE 1994)

It is normal for children and young people to experience personal difficulties while growing up. In *Mental Health in Your School*, Peter Wilson, the Director of Young Minds reports that between 10 and 20 per cent of children may require help with their mental well-being at some point in time (Wilson 1996).

The term 'mental well-being', or 'mental health' may bring to mind many different types of personal problem. At one extreme, difficulties in the area of mental health are often associated with referral to Child Psychiatrists – cases of eating disorders, and low incidence psychiatric conditions such as childhood schizophrenia. At the other extreme, the term is sometimes used as a medical 'catch all' category to include a range of childhood difficulties – behavioural difficulties such as aggression, non compliance, anger outbursts, as well as anxieties, fears and phobias.

In schools and colleges children and young people who experience behavioural and/or personal adjustment problems are 'categorised' as having emotional and/or behavioural difficulties (EBD).

It is sometimes the case that children who experience *behavioural* difficulties are said to exhibit 'conduct disorders', and are not considered to have mental health problems. The term 'mental health' is reserved for emotional problems: problems in the area of *thinking*, e.g. a poor self image (I'm ugly, stupid, have no friends), and the area of *feeling* – the child experiences excessive anxiety in examination situations, panic attacks in enclosed spaces.

The distinction made between children's *behavioural* difficulties and cognitive *(thinking)* and emotional *(feeling)* difficulties is helpful when assessing the child's problems (see later in chapter 'The assessment and management of anxiety').

However this distinction can be superficial and unhelpful if problems of childhood are seen as *either* behavioural problems or mental health problems. It may be the case that behavioural problems are a manifestation of mental health problems – for example behavioural outbursts may be a consequence of irritability, frustration or anger which in turn are a consequence of family disharmony. Conversely, mental health problems may result from behavioural difficulties – for example, the punitive consequences of disruptive behaviour in school may contribute to pupil *thoughts* of lack of self-worth and *feelings* of hopelessness.

Over the past 20 years or so much has been written advising teachers about how to address pupil behavioural difficulties, e.g. *'Behaviour Modification for the Classroom Teacher'* (Axelrod 1997) and *'Towards Better Behaviour'* (Jolly and McNamara 1994).

The success of teacher endeavours in addressing problem behaviour has two payoffs. First, the behavioural difficulties are reduced or eliminated. Second, the possibility of the development of secondary emotional difficulties (mental health problems) is prevented.

The development and availability of teacher resources to respond to pupil behavioural difficulties has not been paralleled by the development of equivalent resources to address mental health problems – although a recent guide for teachers and others working in schools has been published (Wilson 1996). This chapter is a contribution to redress this imbalance; thus the overriding aim is to raise teacher awareness and knowledge about the nature of anxiety, its incidence, assessment and management.

If it is normal for children and young people to experience emotional difficulties when growing up then a question that must be asked is: 'When are such difficulties *not normal* to the extent that they need to be considered as a problem which needs to be addressed?' This and related questions are addressed by exploring some of the relevant theory in the subject area and by demonstrating how the theory has been most useful in developing a range of tools and techniques which are of value to the professional helper. Case studies are included which give practical guidance on the application of the techniques to which reference is made in the text.

## WHAT IS ANXIETY?

Anxiety encompasses

(a) feelings of apprehension and fear;
(b) physiological symptoms such as increased heart rate, tremors, dizziness;
(c) escape and avoidance behaviour;
(d) negative thoughts, e.g. 'I can't cope with this', 'I know I'm going to fail'.

The terms *anxiety, fear, phobia* and *panic* are often used interchangeably – not only by the layman but by professionals. For example, a phobia can be considered to be an extreme form of fear. Sometimes fear is distinguished from a phobia in that the source and cause of the fear can be explicitly identified – a child may be afraid of dogs to a 'debilitating extent' in that the child has hysterics when a dog on a lead passes on the opposite side of the road. The cause may be traced back to when a 'friendly' dog jumped up on the child and attempted to lick his face. In contrast a phobia is sometimes described as an 'irrational fear', i.e. the cause may be unknown. However this distinction is somewhat crude and arbitrary and exceptions to it are not difficult to identify. For example, a pupil may present as school phobic, and enquiries might reveal that

– the child was inclined to be anxious (trait anxiety), also that
– the child was shouted at for not having his PE kit, and was accused of deliberately 'forgetting' his kit in order to avoid the PE lesson, and
– the 'natural' anxiety experienced by the child generalised from the specific incident to the PE lesson, other lessons, school in general and the thought of school ('anticipatory anxiety').

Fears and phobias are best considered as specific examples of anxiety determined behaviours and these two terms can be used interchangeably. In addition to these two a number of other types of anxiety problems have been identified, e.g. separation anxiety and generalised anxiety.

### Normal and abnormal anxiety responses

Anxiety may be a perfectly normal response to stress. In stress situations anxiety prepares the body for action. At times of stress adrenaline is released into the body and the physiological arousal contributes to enhanced physical and psychological performance.

The relationship between an individual's efficiency of performance and level of arousal (stress/anxiety) is illustrated in Figure 6.1.

The level of anxiety/arousal/stress associated with optimum performance varies from one individual to another. For example, in Figure 6.2 optimum performance for John is associated with a relatively low level of arousal while for Janet the converse is the case.

### *Individual differences*

Anxiety is a normal response to stress situations and is a helpful adaptive response to the extent that anxiety facilitates performance in that stress situation.

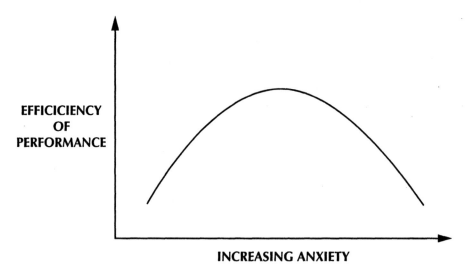

**Figure 6.1** The relationship between anxiety and efficiency of performance

### *The experience of anxiety*

Anxiety can be an unpleasant emotional state. In extreme forms it involves feelings of apprehension and physiological arousal such as palpitations and sweating. The experience of extreme anxiety is similar to that of fear but occurs in the absence of an obvious external threat.

All individuals experience anxiety. Some have a disposition to perceive a wide range of situations as threatening while others do not. This aspect of a person's disposition is referred to as *trait anxiety*. Individuals prone to trait anxiety tend to experience more bouts of anxiety on a day to day basis – known as *state anxiety* – than individuals not so predisposed.

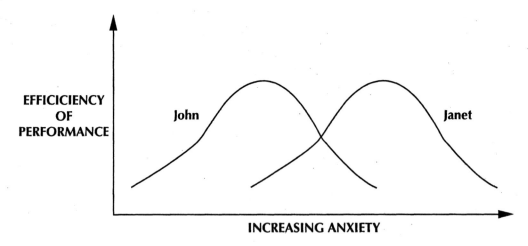

**Figure 6.2** Anxiety and performance: individual differences

## Dimensions and indicators of anxiety

There are three dimensions to anxiety. They are:

(i)     maladaptive behaviours
(ii)    physical symptoms
(iii)   worrying thoughts.

### *Behaviour*

The most common reaction to anxiety is *avoidance* or *escape*. However anxiety can also result in disrupted learning or memory, and in behaviours such as stuttering, sleeplessness, hyperactivity and repetitive behaviours.

### *Physical symptoms*

These are wide ranging and can include stomach-aches, nausea, headaches, palpitations, muscular tension and hot flushes.

### *Worrying thoughts*

Worrying thoughts often contribute to *anticipatory anxiety*. For example, a pupil who experiences anxiety about group discussions might be thinking 'What will I say?' 'What if I say something stupid?' 'Every one will laugh at me', 'What will I do if they laugh?'

## WHEN IS ANXIETY A PROBLEM?

Assuming that anxiety is a normal response and that individuals vary with respect to anxiety-proneness, a second question can be asked, namely 'When is anxiety not a helpful, adaptive response?' Anxiety is not a helpful, adaptive response when the level of anxiety is such that performance in the stress situation is not enhanced but deteriorates or disintegrates.

Before going on to describe the Anxiety Assessment Checklist, consideration is given to the notions of fear, phobia and panic.

## FEAR, PHOBIA AND PANIC

### Fear

This is a normal reaction to real or imagined threatening situations. Surveys of the incidence of childhood fears have been carried out. For young children the data have come from parental reports while for older children the data have come from self reports.

Survey reports found a variable incidence of childhood fears: for example, children aged 2 to 6 years had an average of 4.6 fears and displayed a fear reaction every 4½ days. In contrast, an average of 11 fears was reported by children aged 8 to 11 years. Thus childhood fears are very common, and children report experiencing multiple fears.

In the light of the above conclusion a reasonable question to ask is: 'When should a childhood fear be considered a problem?' In responding to this question three subsidiary questions need to be asked. They are:

(i)     Is the fear debilitating?
(ii)    Is the intensity of the fear response extreme?
(iii)   Is the duration of the fear response overly long?

If the answer to any of the above questions is 'yes', then the assumption that the fear is 'developmentally normal', should be dismissed and the fear should be actively addressed.

## Phobia

A phobia is sometimes considered as a special form of fear. The following characteristics are commonly associated with phobic conditions:

- out of proportion to the demands of the situation
- cannot be explained or reasoned away
- is beyond voluntary control
- leads to avoidance of the fear situation
- persists over an extended period of time
- is unadaptive
- is not age or stage specific, i.e. is not 'developmentally normal'.

## Panic

A panic attack is usually sudden in onset and comprises intense feelings of apprehension and impending disaster. A wide variety of physiological symptoms may be associated with the panic attack:

- shortness of breath or smothering sensations
- dizziness, unsteadiness or fainting
- palpitations or heart rate speeding up
- trembling or shaking
- sweating
- choking
- feeling nauseous
- feeling unreal or 'depersonalised'
- numbness or tingling feelings
- hot flushes
- chest pain or discomfort
- fear of dying
- fear of going crazy or doing something outrageous.

Many authorities consider hyperventilation (rapid shallow breathing) to be a core feature of panic. This hyperventilation can cause over-oxygenation of the blood: this in turn can give rise to physical symptoms such as dizziness, blurred vision, palpitations, breathlessness.

Before prevention and intervention strategies are attempted for anxious children *normal fears and anxieties* must be differentiated from *anxiety disorders* so that unnecessary interventions can be avoided. The following two scenarios clarify the distinction between normal and clinical anxiety.

1. David, a 13-year-old middle set student, always feels nervous before examinations. He says he has 'butterflies in the stomach' and worries if he will pass.

   David always performs adequately in examinations – particularly so when one considers the small amount of revision he undertakes.

   The anxiety David experiences is normal – it is not extensive, nor is it disruptive of performance or adjustment.

2. In contrast to David, James has severe anxiety problems. James, an able 12-year-old student, has always got on well at school. On a morning that James was to make a presentation to a Geography class he refused to go to school and locked himself in the bathroom. Eventually James was coerced into the car, crying hysterically, and after spending an hour with the school nurse was sufficiently calm to go to his classes. In the class in which he was to make his presentation James felt bilious and as his turn to make a presentation approached he left the class to vomit. It was reported that James had experienced similar problems, though less severe, when required to make a presentation in the English class earlier in the year.

   James' difficulties with making public presentations can be considered as 'clinical anxiety' and therefore as warranting attention – for the anxiety is so intense that it is disruptive of performance and adjustment.

### The Anxiety Assessment Checklist

This Checklist, presented as Figure 6.3, is designed for completion by, for example, the pupil's teacher(s) in order to draw together concerns about the pupil's adjustment and situation in order to make a judgement about whether or not the pupil's behaviour and disposition should or should not be considered a problem.

## ANXIETY PROBLEMS IN CHILDHOOD AND ADOLESCENCE

Fears and anxieties are a normal part of child development. Many children's fears and anxieties are temporary, appear in children of similar ages and are not dysfunctional in that they do not interfere with everyday functioning. Such fears and anxieties can be considered 'developmentally normal'.

In contrast to normal fears a child or adolescent may experience a fear that is not age related and which may be interfering with the child's everyday functioning.

### Developmentally normal fears

A review of the reported incidence of fears in childhood allow some generalisations about the nature and incidence of such fears to be made (see Table 6.1).

### Anxiety Assessment Checklist

1.  What are the symptoms/indicators of anxiety?

    i) _____

    ii) _____

    iii) _____

2.  How do the symptoms seem in comparison with the rest of the class?

    i)   symptom 1.   common        uncommon       very rare      never seen before

    ii)  symptom 2.   common        uncommon       very rare      never seen before

    iii) symptom 3.   common        uncommon       very rare      never seen before

3.  Does the pupil currently *generally* present as a nervous/anxious child?      yes/no
    If *no,* When did the pupil begin to present as an anxious/nervous child?

    _____

    _____

    _____

    Can the onset of the anxiety be associated with any particular incident or change
    at home or school?      yes/no
    If *yes,* please *describe* _____

    _____

    _____

4.  To what extent does the pupil's anxiety interfere with:-

    i)   school work              hardly at all        significantly        grossly

    ii)  home work                hardly at all        significantly        grossly

    iii) peer friendships         hardly at all        significantly        grossly

    iv)  family relationships     hardly at all        significantly        grossly

5.  Can the pupil talk to you about his/her anxiety?

    yes, comfortably     yes, with some     no, cannot verbalise     no, becomes agitated
                          difficulty              his/her feelings            and distressed

6.  In what lessons or situations does the pupil display extreme anxiety responses?

    i) _____

    ii) _____

    iii) _____

7.  In what situations does the pupil present as assured and confident?

    i) _____

    ii) _____

    iii) _____

Name of the person completing the Checklist _____

Position _____ Date _____

**Figure 6.3** Anxiety Assessment Checklist

**Table 6.1** Nature and incidences of fears in childhood

| Age | Nature of fears |
| --- | --- |
| 0–6 months | loss of support, loud noises |
| 7–12 months | fear of strangers |
| 1 year | parental separation, sudden, unexpected and looming objects |
| 2 years | loud noises (e.g. vacuum cleaners), animals (e.g. large dogs), dark room |
| 3–5 years | masks, the dark, separation from parents, animals, 'bad' people |
| 6–8 years | ghosts/witches, thunder and lightning, being alone, bodily injury |
| 9–12 years | tests and examinations, school performance, bodily injury, physical injury, thunder and lightning |

Although numerous studies have been carried out on the developmental nature of children's fears and related anxieties, relatively few studies have been published that focus specifically on the prevalence and incidence of school related fears. The research that has been carried out has tended to focus on *school phobia, social withdrawal* (in younger children), and *examination anxiety.* These are the three major fear categories that occur in the school setting and are described below.

## School related fears

### School phobia

This fear of school and associated anxiety prevents children from attending school. This fear can suddenly appear or can be longstanding in nature. The incidence of school phobia has been estimated to occur in between 3 to 17 per cent of school children. In the author's experience it is likely that the 'true' figure is at the lower end of this range. School phobia appears to be most in evidence at the time

- children begin to attend school – often associated with separation anxiety
- at times of school transfer, e.g. from primary to secondary school, and
- at the age of about 14 years – often occuring with depression, but this is of very low frequency of occurrence.

While the above generalisations can be made it should be recognised that school phobia can develop at any age.

### Social withdrawal

This term is used to describe situations in which children avoid interaction with their peers and sometimes refuse to talk in the classroom. The incidence of this has been estimated to range between 10 to 20 per cent, although in the author's experience it occurs at much lower levels than these. Incidence of complete non talking in school (selective/elective mutism) are extremely rare.

### Examination anxiety

This involves the interruption and/or prevention of taking examinations as a result of factors such as excessive worry about one's examination performance, sleep disruption, memory lapses, fear of failure and/or heightened physiological arousal. Incidence figures for test anxiety range from 10 to 30 per cent. Again, in the author's experience, the 'true' figure may be at or below the lower end of the range quoted.

Although most fear studies have found girls to have more fears than boys, this does not seem to be the case with specific school related fears and anxieties.

## THE ASSESSMENT AND MANAGEMENT OF ANXIETY

Anxiety symptoms in young children are usually first identified by the children's parents or teachers. Parents and teachers have to make judgements about the anxiety, in particular as to whether it is 'developmentally normal' or problematic i.e. 'clinical anxiety'. The Anxiety Assessment Checklist, provided earlier in this chapter, is an aid to teachers when making an assessment of their concerns regarding a pupil's anxieties and/or fears. Teachers are able to consult with Educational Psychologists regarding their concerns. Parents have a larger number of professionals with whom they can consult, e.g. Health Visitors, General Practitioners and, in 'serious' cases, Clinical Psychologists.

### Assessment

In the USA two scales have been used to assess fears and anxieties. These are the *Manifest Anxiety Scale* (Reynolds and Richmond 1978) and the *Fear Survey Schedule for Children* (Ollendick 1983). These are useful research instruments to investigate the incidence of fears and anxiety in children. Sometimes they are used to evaluate the effectiveness of intervention by arranging for them to be completed before and after intervention. However such scales and surveys are rather blunt instruments when assessing an individual child's situation.

Probably the most efficient method for assessing anxiety problems in children and adolescents is to simply ask the young person about them. For young children such an interview is augmented by parental interview information – the more so the younger the child.

### The assessment interview

When conducting an assessment interview with the child and parent(s) it is important to ensure that the child is the focus of the interview. In other words information about the problem(s) is elicited from the child. It may well be that the interviewer will wish to draw on parental observations about the child's reports of behaviours, perceptions, beliefs, and problematic situations. However the interviewer should always try to reach an agreement about the structure of the interview with the parent(s) before it is commenced. The agreement aimed for might be:

(a) That the interview will be conducted with the child as the prime interviewee.
(b) The parent(s) should give a non-verbal signal if they wish to make a contribution e.g. a raised index finger.

(c) The parent(s) should wait for the interviewer to invite them to make the contribution.

(d) The interviewer will indicate to the parent(s) if he or she wishes the parent(s) to expand, modify, qualify, explain or comment on any of the child's responses.

The reasons for the above structure to the interview are as follows:

(a) The child's perception, beliefs and evaluation of his or her situation are the starting point for intervention. The child's perceptions, beliefs and evaluations may or may not be accurate but they must be assessed and recorded. If the parent(s) feel that inaccurate or 'false' information is being elicited from the child then they may attempt to 'correct' the child during the course of the interview. Such interruptions can be obstructive to obtaining an accurate assessment of 'the problems' as perceived and experienced by the child.

(b) The interviewer needs to be aware that the parent(s) wish to contribute to the interview.

(c) The interviewer can invite the parental contribution at a time during the interview that is not disruptive of the child's contribution.

(d) The interviewer may wish to have corroboration of what the child has said or to obtain more information than can be elicited from the child.

The author arrived at the above interview structure as in clinical practice he had experienced particularly fruitful periods of the interview with the child being disrupted by parent interjections.

The *aims of the interview* are to identify:

(i)     the specific manifestations of the child's anxiety;
(ii)    the situations in which the anxiety is exhibited;
(iii)   its history and intensity;
(iv)    the circumstances which constrain or exacerbate it.

These aims focus on achieving an accurate assessment of the behavioural dimensions of the problem – for there is an extensive literature reporting successful responses to anxiety problems using behavioural approaches such as *systematic desensitisation* and *relaxation training* (see later sections 'Progressive muscle relaxation' and 'Avoidance').

However, there are other dimensions to the problems associated with debilitating anxiety, namely thoughts and feelings (see 'What is anxiety?' earlier in chapter). These dimensions too need to be assessed so that a comprehensive assessment of the contributory factors to the anxiety state can be achieved. Such a comprehensive assessment facilitates intervention responses which are complimentary to the behavioural approaches. The more significant contributory factors include:

(i)     *negative self-talk:* 'I'll never be able to go to school again', 'I'm rubbish at school work', 'Nobody likes me', 'I'm bound to fail this exam';
(ii)    *misinterpretation:* of life events, for example after feeling they had made a complete mess of a maths homework the pupil concludes.

(a) 'I'll never be any good at maths' – ignoring that the previous year they had obtained a B Grade on an A to E scale

(b) 'I'm no good at maths' – failing to take into account that the three previous maths homeworks had been marked as 'Very good', 'Good' and 'Well done!' respectively

(c) 'I'm no good at school work' – i.e. over-generalising from one specific subject area

(d) 'If I'm not brilliant at maths I must be rubbish at maths' – believing that one has either to be very good at maths or is very poor at maths, when in reality the pupil may be average at maths

(e) 'I must be stupid' – assuming that poor performance was due to a *personal shortcoming* – whereas the reality is that the lesson on which the homework was based had been poorly taught by a student teacher.

The above examples of 'distorted' thinking are not uncommonly associated with problems of anxiety: indeed these types of distorted thinking are so prevalent as contributory factors to anxiety states that six common *systematic errors in logical thinking* have been identified. These errors are defined and described in Table 6.2. The above examples (a) to (e) are illustrative of five of these common errors in thinking. These are:

(a) magnification
(b) selective abstraction
(c) over-generalisation
(d) dichotomous thinking
(e) personalisation.

Scrutiny of the examples (ii, a to e) above reveal that they are not mutually exclusive: most of the examples quoted could fall into more than one of the categories described Table 6.2. The interventions to address problems caused by systematic errors in logical thinking aim to challenge and refute these errors (see next section 'Intervention'). It is a matter of judgement for the counsellor (or

**Table 6.2** Systematic errors in logical thinking

| | |
|---|---|
| 1. Arbitrary inference | A tendency to arbitrarily conclude from one event to another event which is not justified by the facts of the situation. |
| 2. Over-generalisation | A tendency to conclude from one event to other events without adequate information. |
| 3. Selective abstraction | A tendency to consider a complex event on the basis of one aspect of it. |
| 4. Magnification and minimisation | A tendency to exaggerate negative events and minimise positive ones. |
| 5. Personalisation | A tendency to assume responsibiity for an event (usually negative) when there is no basis for doing so. |
| 6. Dichotomous thinking | A tendency to evaluate events in extreme categories. |

teacher) to identify the most appropriate categorisation of the 'thinking error'. Usually this is the categorisation judged easiest to challenge.

The premise that 'faulty thinking' causes 'faulty behaviour', or, put another way, dysfunctional thinking causes dysfunctional behaviour, is the basic premise underlying cognitive therapy. A number of common dysfunctional beliefs that are held by children have been identified. It is helpful to bear these in mind during the diagnostic interview with the child – for the professional can then explore with the child whether any of these dysfunctional beliefs are contributing to the child's anxiety. These common dysfunctional beliefs include:

It's bad if I make a mistake.
It's awful if others don't like me.
I should always get what I want.
Things should come easy to me.
The world should be fair and bad people should be punished.
I shouldn't show my feelings.
Adults should be perfect.
There's only one right answer.
I must win.
I shouldn't have to wait for anything.

### Intervention: the self-management of anxiety

No person can manage another person's anxiety. The management of anxiety is essentially *self-management*. Obviously, the younger the child the more help and support the child requires in order to be able to 'self-manage'. The role of the helper, be it teacher, parent or professional therapist, is multidimensional. The dimensions include:

(a) helping the child understand their anxiety;
(b) communicating to the child that the anxiety can be managed;
(c) when possible, offering choices of strategies to cope with the anxiety;
(d) offering skill training when skills are required to manage the anxiety.

The assessment of the presenting symptoms of anxiety forms the starting point from which to formulate the focus of intervention.

The relationship between presenting symptoms and focus of interventions is presented in Table 6.3.

### Progressive muscle relaxation

Relaxation provides relief from physical and mental tension. It is often the first skill to be taught to the anxious person. This is because progressive muscle relaxation is:

(a) easy to learn;
(b) has credibility for the anxious person;
(c) can be readily applied in anxiety provoking situations.

**Table 6.3** The relationship between presenting symptoms and focus of interventions

| Presenting symptoms | Treatment focus |
| --- | --- |
| Tension, palpitations, shaking | Progressive muscle relaxation and deep breathing |
| Avoidance | Gradual exposure |
| Worrying thoughts and distorted thinking | Positive self-instruction and challenging distortions |
| Panic attacks | Panic prevention and management e.g. slow, deep breathing |

The young person is first taught how to relax all the muscle groups in turn and to become more sensitive to the difference between tense and relaxed states. A full progressive muscle relaxation routine can take up to half an hour.

Once the full routine has been fully mastered the routine is significantly shortened – by selectively focusing on the relaxation practices. Finally the young person is taught to associate the relaxed state with the mental image of a relaxed, serene situation (a quiet beach, a glade in a wood, floating in a hot air balloon).

In summary, the child is taught a programme of relaxation training that is progressively shortened until it can be drawn on by the child in preparation for or actually in the anxiety provoking situation.

Some schools provide relaxation classes for GCSE students (see Duffy 1992). Students are taught progressive muscle relaxation routines, breathing exercises and visualisation techniques . . .' Imagine you are on a warm sunny beach with waves lapping backwards and forwards . . .' The result is that the students are calm and relaxed in examination situations and consequently perform better.

## Avoidance

When a situation is a source of anxiety (for example, at school), the easiest and most effective short-term response is to avoid the situation. This response results in avoidance of the aversive (unpleasant) situation. However this short-term 'effective' response has medium- and long-term negative consequences. First, dysfunctional behaviour (non school attendance) is negatively reinforced. An implication of this is that this inappropriate behavioural response to the anxiety provoking situation is consolidated and becomes harder to overcome. Second, the successful avoidance of the anxiety provoking situation enhances the probability that even thinking about it will elicit *anticipatory anxiety*.

The most effective means of overcoming avoidance is by exposure to the situation that elicits the anxiety/avoidance. Programmes designed to overcome avoidance almost always consist of graded exposure. Graded exposure or *systematic desensitisation* involves breaking the desired behaviour down into its constituent behaviours and identifying a hierarchy of responses from least anxiety provoking to most anxiety provoking. For example the problem of school phobia (i.e. attendance at school), could be broken down as follows:

(i)     Get up and dress in school uniform.

(ii)    Walk around the school dressed in school uniform on Saturday and/or Sunday.

(iii)   Enter the school on a school day.

(iv)    Enter the school and stay on site for progressively longer periods of time.

(v)     Attend one lesson.

(vi)    Progressively attend more and more lessons.

(vii)   Attend all lessons perhaps with some anxiety.

(viii)  Attend all lessons with no anxiety.

The actual steps in any desensitisation programme are mutually agreed with the pupil and may vary from pupil to pupil. The professional helper or teacher should beware of inadvertently hindering rapid progress up the hierarchy by insisting that the pupil take one step at a time. For example the 'school phobia' might in fact turn out to be a case of separation anxiety – and once the pupil is physically separated from the mother and is in school they may readily attend all lessons. Conversely this may not be so (see Case study 1).

Desensitisation in the real-life situation is referred to as *in vivo* desensitisation. This *in vivo* desensitisation can be compared with *imaginal desensitisation*. Imaginal desensitisation involves the pupil following the progressive muscle relaxation routine and, while in this relaxed state, being guided by the professional helper up the hierarchy of anxiety from the minimally anxiety provoking situations to the maximally anxiety provoking situation, while at the same time maintaining the relaxed state.

Some therapists always precede *in vivo* desensitisation by imaginal desensitisation – as an aid to encouraging an anticipation of a successful outcome for the *in vivo* desensitisation. Other therapists only precede *in vivo* desensitisation by imaginal desensitisation if the pupil is judged poorly motivated or too anxious to attempt the *in vivo* desensitisation.

The theoretical basis for the practice of graded exposure is that the association between the feared situation and anxiety is broken. Hence the effectiveness of the graded exposure programme can be enhanced at each step by encouraging the pupil to use the short form of the progressive muscle relaxation programme so that the situation that was associated with anxiety becomes associated with a relaxed state.

## Worrying thoughts and cognitive distortions

There are two stages in the management of worrying thoughts and cognitive distortions. The first stage is the identification of the worrying thoughts and distorted cognitions – usually achieved in the assessment interview: the second stage is the actual management of the worrying thoughts and distorted cognitions.

The two main strategies for *countering* or *controlling* dysfunctional thoughts are *distraction* and *challenging*.

### Distraction

This strategy is based on the assumption that a person can only attend to one thought at a time. Therefore the aim of distraction strategies is to displace the dysfunctional thought – which is anxiety provoking – with a neutral or pleasant thought. Pupils' can be taught this skill in the interview situation. There are three common types of distraction strategies. They are:

(i)    physical activity
(ii)   refocusing
(iii)  formal mental activity.

*Physical activity.* This strategy involves the pupil occupying himself with a 'distracting activity' so that the worrying thoughts are not dwelt upon. For example, a pupil anxious at the beginning of a lesson could be asked to give the books out or be asked to remind the teacher five minutes from the end of the lesson that homework had to be set.

*Refocusing.* This strategy involves the pupil self-selecting a mental activity at the time they begin to worry. For example, in the classroom he or she might be encouraged to count the pictures on the wall, the number of fellow students with their ears covered by their hair.

*Formal mental activity.* This strategy aims to displace the dysfunctional cognitive activity by a 'neutral' cognitive activity. For example, when beginning to dwell on worrying thoughts the pupil can be encouraged to recite a piece of poetry or times tables.

Formal mental activity is similar to refocusing, but whereas formal mental activity involves a predetermined mental activity replacing the worrying thought, refocusing depends on the pupil concentrating hard on a non-threatening aspect of the environment.

### Challenging thoughts

Distraction techniques aim to displace worrying thoughts so that they are no longer present to elicit anxiety. However some people cannot accept distraction techniques as they believe that the content of the worrying thought must be addressed. For these people the content of the worrying thoughts have to be challenged successfully before it can be displaced.

The aim of challenging worrying thoughts is to re-evaluate them and reformulate them constructively. The techniques used to do this can be *rational argument*, i.e. demonstrating the inaccuracy or illogicality of the content of the worrying thought or *empirical refutation*, i.e. supporting the pupil to collect evidence that refutes the worrying thought or cognitive distortion.

In the author's experience the latter strategy is the most effective – for rational argument aimed at encouraging the student to accept that he or she is wrong may either:

(a) be rejected because of the adverse effect accepting would have on self-esteem; or

(b) be accepted but as a consequence result in a lowering of self-esteem and consequent diminution in motivation to change.

## CASE STUDIES

In real-life situations many people successfully cope with (self-manage) anxiety without a theoretical understanding of the different anxiety states and without seeking professional help. They just 'discover' their own way of dealing with personal anxiety. The methods 'discovered' are usually those that would be suggested by professional therapists had their help been sought, i.e. relaxing, deep breathing, imaginal rehearsal, facing up to rather than avoiding anxiety provoking situations.

The previous section of this chapter focused on the assessment and management of anxiety at a theoretical level. Sometimes providing the anxious person with a self-help book containing this sort of information is sufficient to empower the person to self-manage their anxiety. When this does not happen the reason for the 'failure' is often:

(a) having a poor understanding of the rationale of the technique(s) used and little expectation of success;

(b) using a technique inappropriately, incompletely or incorrectly;

(c) having an unrealistically high expectation of the effectiveness of the technique(s) – perhaps believing that anxiety can be *cured* whereas the realistic objective is effective self-management, i.e. *coping* with the anxiety so that it is not debilitating in terms of restricting behaviour or discomforting in terms of personal feelings and disposition.

### The structure of intervention

When helping a young person overcome problems of anxiety the above possibilities have to be borne in mind and addressed so that the intervention has a high probability of a successful outcome.

The first step is to verify the problem formulation with the young person.

The second step is to share with the young person the diaries, records and evaluations of other successful outcome case studies. The reason for presenting examples of successful interventions are that they:

(a) illustrate what has to be done;

(b) show that it can be done;

(c) create an expectation that it will be done;

(d) create an expectation of initial difficulty which is 'normal'

(e) create an expectation of a positive outcome.

This practice strengthens the young person's commitment to an intervention programme, engenders an expectation of success and prepares the young person for the teaching of the actual techniques to be used and the rationale underlying the techniques.

The failure that may result from a technique being used inappropriately, incompletely or incorrectly is avoided by:

(a) teaching the technique(s) in the therapy session(s) *(skill acquisition)*;
(b) negotiating that the young person practice the techniques at home *(homework)*;
(c) negotiating that the young person keeps a record of the homework *(diary record)*.

When an intervention plan has been agreed with the young person: (i) the specific goals of each stage are agreed; and (ii) progress is jointly monitored by the young person and his or her helper. This practice ensures that realistic goals are set and also enables constructive reformulations of 'failure' to be identified – thereby reducing the possibility that the young person will opt out of the programme should a target not be achieved. It is also helpful to explain to the young person that progress may not be smooth and regular but that occasional 'relapses' might occur – and that such relapses are normal and occur less and less as the programme progresses.

There follows some brief case descriptions of the successful self-management of anxiety. They illustrate the methodology and recording techniques used. These cases include:

Case study 1 – School phobia;
Case study 2 – School phobia with depression;
Case study 3 – Generalised anxiety (trait anxiety);
Case study 4 – Generalised anxiety developing into agoraphobia;
Case study 5 – Peer fear (bullying);
Case study 6 – Migraine induced anxiety.

The structure adopted for each case history is as follows:

Background
Diagnostic Interview
Formulation
Intervention
Outcome.

## CASE STUDY 1 – SCHOOL PHOBIA

Margaret was referred by the Health Visitor to the Educational Psychologist. She had been taken to the family GP as she was very distressed before school and refused to attend. The Health Visitor was asked to visit the home to help, and judged that a referral to the Educational Psychologist was appropriate.

The *diagnostic interview* with Margaret and her mother revealed the following:

(i)  Margaret had some 'mild' difficulties attending Primary school the previous term because she had suffered intermittently with bouts of diarrhoea.
(ii)  In a Chemistry lesson during her first week at High School, Margaret had felt sick and had visited the School Nurse.

(iii) The School Nurse had suggested that Margaret rest in the Nurse's room while she (the School Nurse) went to attend to some other matters

(iv) After a while Margaret felt better, but also felt a little anxious as she felt that she had been forgotten.

(v) Margaret decided to leave the Nurse's room and go to her next lesson, music.

(vi) In a corridor, Margaret came across a teacher and asked him the way to the Music room.

(vii) In a very unfriendly voice the teacher responded 'The first thing to learn in this school, girl, is to call me "Sir" '.

(viii) Margaret's difficulties (i.e. anxiety about attending school) escalated after this series of incidents until three or four days later Margaret was unable to attend school – and became very distressed when her mother attempted to insist that she attend.

*Formulation.* Margaret's extreme anxiety about attending school had developed from the 'normal' anxiety associated with the series of incidents described. The anxiety was responded to by avoidance, i.e. not attending school. This successful avoidance (a) reinforced the inappropriate non school attendance behaviour, and (b) created the conditions for anticipatory anxiety to develop, i.e. fear about the thought of attending school.

*Intervention*

(i) Margaret was taught progressive muscle relaxation and deep breathing.

(ii) Margaret was taken through three sessions of imaginal rehearsal, i.e. while in the relaxed state Margaret was asked to imagine getting up, getting dressed in school uniform, walking to school and attending lessons. These sessions were conducted at the local school clinic on a Monday, Wednesday and Friday. The Friday imaginal rehearsal included an 'inoculation therapy' component. Margaret was asked to imagine herself being distressed, crying and being sick, but nonetheless leaving the house and walking to school.

An inoculation therapy component is helpful in that usually it is very difficult for the young person to take the first step in the gradual exposure programme. However, if the young person is led to expect that it will be difficult, the likelihood that the young person will persist in the face of difficulty is enhanced.

(iii) Towards the end of the Friday session is was agreed that Margaret would visit the school and walk around the grounds on both Saturday and Sunday. Margaret also drew up a hierarchy of preferred lessons: from most preferred (English) to least preferred (PE). It was agreed that:

(a) Margaret would attend school on the Monday and spend the time in either the Year Tutor's room or in the Library,

(b) On subsequent days Margaret would attend English lessons and progressively go to more and more lessons – working her way down the hierarchy from most preferred lessons to least preferred.

(iv)   Margaret also kept a record of lesson attendance and initially graphed each day the number of lessons attended (see Figure 6.4).

As the young person makes progress through the graded exposure (systematic desensitisation) programme, the self-recording of the gradual improvement can act as positive reinforcement – as can recognition of the progress by significant others, e.g. teachers, parents, professional helper. The recording of progress also facilitates target setting – the targets are usually agreed by the young person and helper. Target (goal) achievement is also a positive reinforcer. The data as presented in Figure 6.4 is not too amenable to target setting – for it is not uncommon for the number of lessons attended on a given day not to be exceeded by the number of lessons attended on the day following. Therefore to set targets on a daily basis which aimed to 'beat' the number of lessons attended the previous day may have resulted in targets not being met: this in turn may have adversely effected pupil motivation and commitment to the desensitisation programme. However, if the data are collapsed into weekly totals as in Figure 6.5, then:

(a)  steady progression can be seen; and
(b)  targets can be set, e.g. 'See how much you can beat your previous week's total by'.

Historically this graded exposure programme would have been discontinued when full lesson attendance had been achieved and consolidated. However in order to be confident that relapse will not occur when professional support is withdrawn, the 'up to date' intervention would also include an assessment of how the pupil feels during the programme, for if the pupil feels comfortable in lessons, then relapse is less likely than when this is not the case. This case study is fully reported in the literature (McNamara 1988b). The methodology for the assessment of feelings is described in the following case study.

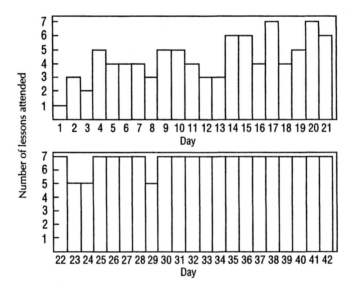

**Figure 6.4** Increase in lesson attendance over a 42-day period

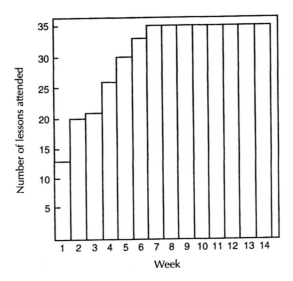

**Figure 6.5** Increase in lesson attendance over a 14-week period

## CASE STUDY 2 – SCHOOL PHOBIA WITH DEPRESSION

David was referred by the Education Welfare Officer (EWO) to the Educational Psychologist. The school had brought David's school attendance difficulties to the EWO's attention. The EWO had called at David's home on a number of mornings to take him to school. On these occasions David was physically sick when on the school premises.

The *diagnostic interview* with David and his mother revealed the following:

(i)      There had been some problems of attendance in the Primary school.
(ii)     David, a second year High School pupil, had not experienced any obvious difficulties in attendance in his first year.
(iii)    David exhibited both chronic diarrhoea and sickness at home before school, and in school when attendance was insisted upon.
(iv)    David had been seen by the GP who had diagnosed depression and had prescribed a course of medication.
(v)     David's mother was physically unwell having heart and lung problems.
(vi)    David's father worked long hours and David's mother exercised most care and control.
(vii)   David wanted to go to school.

*Formulation.* No external causes for David's depression could be identified. It is known that a small number of children exhibiting childhood anxiety problems do go on to develop childhood depression but in David's case no earlier signs of anxiety had been noted. Thus, in contrast to Case study 1 described above, a formulation about the origin and development of the presenting problems could not be constructed.

*Intervention*
(i)     Consultation with the GP took place and it was agreed that medication, monitored by the GP, would continue and that the Educational Psychologist would focus on the school associated difficulties.
(ii)    David was taught progressive muscle relaxation and deep breathing.
(iii)   It was agreed that David would attend school: when at school David would attend lessons when able, and when unable he would work in the foyer near to the secretary's office. David kept a record of school and lesson attendance (Figure 6.6).

Using progressive muscle relaxation and deep breathing as the main anxiety self-management strategies, David was successful in attending up to 50 per cent of lessons each day – almost all of which were before the lunch break.

*Further problem analysis.* David reported that even when he attended lessons he felt awful. He also reported that although he had permission to leave lessons if he couldn't cope, nonetheless some teachers attempted to persuade and cajole him to stay when he wished to exit – and this precipitated panic.

---

**DAY No: 5**

**REPORT BY DAVID ON THE SCHOOL DAY** _____
Arrived at School at _____ *8.55* _____
Registration Period/Assembly _____ *Attended* _____
Period 1 _____ *Attended* _____
Period 2 _____ *Attended* _____
Period 3 _____ *Attended* _____
Period 4 _____ *Attended* _____
Lunch Period _____ *Had lunch* _____
Period 5 _____ *worked outside office* _____
Period 6 _____ *worked outside office* _____
Period 7 _____ *worked outside office* _____
Period 8 _____ *worked outside office* _____
Homework Assignments _____ *Maths* _____

---

**Figure 6.6** School and lesson attendance record

*Modified intervention*
(i)     Each day David was given written permission to leave a lesson on request and was asked to show the slip of paper to each teacher at the beginning of each lesson – (Figure 6.7).
(ii)    David was informed about the nature of panic and it was agreed that he would attempt panic control strategies, i.e. deep, slow breathing and refocusing.
(iii)   A modified self-assessment sheet was instituted (Figure 6.8).

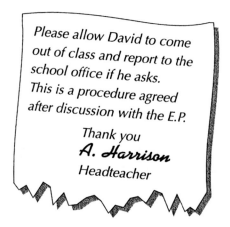

Please allow David to come out of class and report to the school office if he asks.
This is a procedure agreed after discussion with the E.P.
Thank you
*A. Harrison*
Headteacher

**Figure 6.7** 'Lesson exit' slip

## RECORD OF SELF CONFIDENCE

Scale: 100% = at ease, enjoyed lesson.
50% = neither particularly happy nor particularly upset.
0% = upset, felt sick, worried.

Week beginning __8/9/97__

| | Mon. | ✓ or X | % | Tues. | ✓ or X | % | Wed. | ✓ or X | % | Thurs. | ✓ or X | % | Frid. | ✓ or X | % |
|---|---|---|---|---|---|---|---|---|---|---|---|---|---|---|---|
| 1 | Euro. Stud. | ✓ | 5% | English | ✓ | 5% | French | ✓ | 5% | Games | ✓ | 21% | French | ✓ | 8% |
| 2 | Euro. Stud. | ✓ | 5% | English | ✓ | 5% | French | ✓ | 5% | Games | ✓ | 21% | Maths | ✓ | 6% |
| 3 | Music | ✓ | 1% | Maths | ✓ | 2% | Geography | ✓ | 1% | R.E. | ✓ | 21% | Art | ✓ | 8% |
| 4 | French | ✓ | 1% | Maths | ✓ | 10% | Geography | ✓ | 5% | R.E. | ✓ | 5% | Art | ✓ | 3% |
| 5 | Science | ✓ | 2% | Games | ✓ | 2% | Art | ✓ | 21% | Maths | ✓ | 5% | English | ✓ | 1% |
| 6 | Science | ✓ | 1% | Games | ✓ | 21% | Art | ✓ | 21% | Tutorial | ✓ | 5% | English | ✓ | 2% |
| 7 | Music | ✓ | 2% | History | ✓ | 21% | Euro. Stud. | ✓ | 5% | English | ✓ | 3% | Science | ✓ | 1% |
| 8 | Drama | ✓ | 1% | History | ✓ | 5% | Maths | ✓ | 4% | Italian | ✓ | 5% | Science | ✓ | 1% |

**I certify that this is an honest judgement of my self confidence in lessons.**

Signed ..........*David Banks*..........

**Figure 6.8** A completed protocol for the assessment of lesson attendance and self-confidence

The data recorded by David provided material which could be used to tackle David's 'awful' feelings during lessons. This was done by using the data to facilitate positive restructuring on David's part. Examples of strategies used to promote higher self-confidence and correspondingly lower anxiety are described below.

1. Feedback the fact of lesson(s) attendance with the interpretation: 'This shows that you are overcoming your anxiety'.

2. Promote an expectation of increased self-confidence: 'This [overcoming your anxiety] will soon be reflected in your self-assessments'.

3. Promote an expectation of improvement sooner rather than later – but not in a way that indicates failure if it doesn't materialise: e.g. 'most people show improvement after a week, but some take a bit longer: I can't wait until Friday to see how you are getting on'.

4. Ask questions about lessons: attempt to elicit responses which can lead to the pupil reassessing self-confidence and perhaps re-evaluating the lesson more positively. For example:

*Teacher:*  What happened in French for you to rate it 5 per cent?
*Pupil:*  Miss told me off for not drawing a margin down the side of the page.
*Teacher:*  Did anything else happen?
*Pupil:*  No.
*Teacher:*  Was everything else in the lesson OK?
*Pupil:*  Yes.
*Teacher:*  If an average lesson is 50 per cent and the only thing that happened was the thing about the margin, is a 5 per cent rating a bit too low?
*Pupil:*  Yes.
*Teacher:*  What do you think a more accurate rating would be?
*Pupil:*  About 30 per cent.
*Teacher:*  Do you want to change it to 30 per cent?
*Pupil:*  Yes.
*Teacher:*  On Monday you assessed both Science and Music as 2 per cent.
*Pupil:*  Yes.
*Teacher:*  If one lesson was worse than the other, which one would it be?
*Pupil:*  Music.
*Teacher:*  So Science was better?
*Pupil:*  Yes.
*Teacher:*  A lot better?
*Pupil:*  Well, a bit better.
*Teacher:*  If Music was 2 per cent how would you rate Science?
*Pupil:*  I'm not sure.
*Teacher:*  Five per cent more or 50 per cent more?
*Pupil:*  Well, maybe 10 per cent.
*Teacher:*  So we change our rating of Science to . . . ?"
*Pupil:*  10 per cent.

Over an eight week period the use of strategies such as those described above contributed to a successful change in the pupil's self-reported self-confidence in lessons – an improvement spontaneously commented on by subject teachers. Week 8 self-assessment data are presented in Figure 6.9.

*Time commitment.* Initially the management of anxiety demands significant input from the professional helper; sometimes every other day for two weeks, and then less frequent face to face contact as progress is made. Good use can be made of telephone contact and written communications. When a professional

## RECORD OF SELF CONFIDENCE

Scale: 100% = at ease, enjoyed lesson.
50% = neither particularly happy nor particularly upset.
0% = upset, felt sick, worried.

Week beginning *13/10/97*

| | Mon. | ✓ or ✗ | % | Tues. | ✓ or ✗ | % | Wed. | ✓ or ✗ | % | Thurs. | ✓ or ✗ | % | Frid. | ✓ or ✗ | % |
|---|---|---|---|---|---|---|---|---|---|---|---|---|---|---|---|
| 1 | Euro. Stud. | ✓ | 93% | English | ✓ | 91% | French | ✓ | 90% | Games | ✓ | 99% | French | ✓ | 99% |
| 2 | Euro. Stud. | ✓ | 92% | English | ✓ | 99% | French | ✓ | 99% | Games | ✓ | 100% | Maths | ✓ | 89% |
| 3 | Music | ✓ | 100% | Maths | ✓ | 99% | Geography | ✓ | 100% | R.E. | ✓ | 100% | Art | ✓ | 100% |
| 4 | French | ✓ | 91% | Maths | ✓ | 90% | Geography | ✓ | 100% | R.E. | ✓ | 100% | Art | ✓ | 100% |
| 5 | Science | ✓ | 99% | Games | ✓ | 100% | Art | ✓ | 100% | Maths | ✓ | 100% | English | ✓ | 100% |
| 6 | Science | ✓ | 98% | Games | ✓ | 100% | Art | ✓ | 100% | Tutorial | ✓ | 100% | English | ✓ | 100% |
| 7 | Music | ✓ | 100% | History | ✓ | 100% | Euro. Stud. | ✓ | 100% | English | ✓ | 100% | Science | ✓ | 100% |
| 8 | Drama | ✓ | 100% | History | ✓ | 99% | Maths | ✓ | 100% | Italian | ✓ | 99% | Science | ✓ | 100% |

**I certify that this is an honest judgement of my self confidence in lessons.**

Signed ......*David Banks*......................

**Figure 6.9** Improvements in self-assessment of self-confidence

helper writes to a young person in a positive vein this is reinforcing to the young person – and every time the young person looks at the letter it can act as a cue for the young person to self-reinforce. Often the young person may spontaneously pin the positive communication on their bedroom wall. Examples of 'case work correspondence' are illustrated in Figures 6.10(a) to 6.10(c).

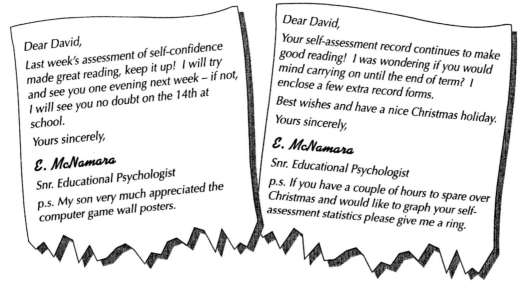

Dear David,
Last week's assessment of self-confidence made great reading, keep it up! I will try and see you one evening next week – if not, I will see you no doubt on the 14th at school.
Yours sincerely,

*E. McNamara*
Snr. Educational Psychologist
p.s. My son very much appreciated the computer game wall posters.

Dear David,
Your self-assessment record continues to make good reading! I was wondering if you would mind carrying on until the end of term? I enclose a few extra record forms.
Best wishes and have a nice Christmas holiday.
Yours sincerely,

*E. McNamara*
Snr. Educational Psychologist
p.s. If you have a couple of hours to spare over Christmas and would like to graph your self-assessment statistics please give me a ring.

**6.10(a)** Positive written feedback to the young person

**6.10(b)** Further positive written feedback to the young person

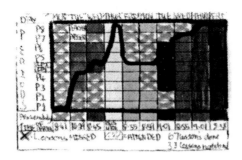

**6.10(c)** Positive written feedback from the headteacher to the professional helper!

The following four brief case study descriptions are presented to illustrate varying implementation strategies used to encourage commitment to the self-management intervention from the young person, and to sustain and reinforce continued programme compliance.

## CASE STUDY 3 – GENERALISED ANXIETY (TRAIT ANXIETY)

James, in his second year at High School, was referred to the Educational Psychologist in June by the school at his mother's request. The referral read: 'James is unhappy at school. He is not eating properly and constantly gets headaches. His mother would prefer to educate him at home.' James was missing some school, showing signs of distress before attending school, and in school presented as a nervous and anxious young man.

Prior to the diagnostic interview, Junior school records were scrutinised. The following summary of James' disposition just prior to transferring to High School was recorded. 'James is an extremely quiet, shy and sensitive boy who easily displays his emotions. He has ability but is nervous of doing things wrong and needs a great deal of encouragement'.

The *diagnostic interview* with James and his mother revealed the following:

(i)  James wakes up about 8.00 a.m. and the first thing he thinks about is 'What day is it and what have I got in school?'

(ii)  James feels sick when he wakes up and doesn't eat or drink anything before he goes to school.

(iii)  James goes home at lunch time and has a bag of chips for lunch – returning to school in the afternoon.

(iv)  James had suffered from migraine from the age of five – when his father had died.

(v)  James reported that noise in school brought on headaches/migraine.

(vi)  The worst time for James was swimming lessons, the noise, squealing and smell.

(vii)  James also became upset when teachers raised their voice, even if James was not the target pupil(s).

(viii)  James was perhaps more distressed outside of lessons than in lessons: arrangements had been made for James to use the Library as a sanctuary, but sometimes prefects 'didn't believe him' and wouldn't allow him access.

*Formulation.* James evidenced trait anxiety – he was anxious, and in addition specific situations could be identified which precipitated severe anxiety.

*Intervention*

(i)  James was taught progressive muscle relaxation techniques: he was lent an audiocassette of the muscle relaxation routine and agreed to follow the procedure twice a day and to keep a record of this homework.

(ii)  James was provided with a note indicating that he had permission to go to the library when he wished.

(iii)  Over the Summer holiday at a support session meeting it was agreed with James that an appropriate strategy when he was beginning to feel anxious in class was to think of something nice.

(iv)  James was provided with two different commercially available relaxation cassettes: he was asked to use them both and to choose which one helped him to relax best James was then to use the chosen tape (see Figure 6.11.).

*Outcome.* After a little over a week James had identified his 'favourite' tape and wrote 'I can imagine walking through the woods without the tape now'. James commenced the Autumn term and when feeling anxious in lessons was able to refocus on the contents of the pleasurable tape. He was also able to access the library out of lesson time if he felt the need.

James attended the first seven weeks of the term without any absences. Later in the term James' mother, who initiated the referral, indicated that she felt that professional support for James was no longer required. She reported that:

(i)  James was doing fine;

(ii)  James was volunteering statements such as 'school's not so bad, mum';

(iii)  James' migraine attacks had fallen to one or two per month (from one or two per week) and that the severity of the attacks had decreased significantly.

## CASE STUDY 4 – GENERALISED ANXIETY DEVELOPING INTO AGORAPHOBIA

Mark, who had an uneventful career at Primary school, transferred to Secondary school successfully. A month or so into the Autumn term when Mark was walking

| Date | Relaxation tape | | Comments |
|---|---|---|---|
| | yes/no | time | Best side: Brown tape, side two |
| Wednesday 14th | yes | 9 pm | Side one, brown tape made me feel tingly and warm. |
| Thursday 15th | yes | 8am, 4pm, 9pm | Side one again. Side two is my favourite side especially visualising different scenes. |
| Friday 16th | yes | 8 am, 8.15 pm | Listen to side two scenes ① listening to favourite music ② In the log cabin ③ Walking through the wood. |
| Saturday 17th | No | – | – |
| Sunday 18th | yes | 8.15 am, 9 pm | I prefer the man's deep soft voice to the woman's voice in the green tape. |
| Monday 19th | yes | 8.00 am, 9 pm | The man's voice is nice and soft and soothing. |
| Tuesday 20th | yes | 8 am, 9 pm | I can imagine walking through the woods without the tape now. |

**Figure 6.11** Diary record of homework assignment

home from school, a car drew up near to him and the driver beckoned him over. Mark became very alarmed and frightened and ran into a nearby shop where he cried hysterically. Shortly afterwards Mark had two panic attacks. The first when he was in a leisure complex with a friend and his parents. His parents indicated that they intended to visit a shop next door and would be away for 15 or 20 minutes. Mark became hysterical at the thought of being left by his parents. On the second occasion, Mark was with his parents and some friends at a bowling alley. Mark's parents were going to the kiosk, some 20 yards away, to buy some refreshments. Mark became hysterical and insisted that one of his parents stay with him. Mark then began to exhibit anxiety about leaving home on his own, e.g. to go to a friend's house or the shops. Previously he had been able to do both without any concerns.

*Formulation.* Mark's anxiety about going out alone, and panicking when he felt he was being left alone (albeit with other youngsters of his own age), was a development from the fear-eliciting incident with the man in the car.

*Intervention*

(i)    The theory underlying the development of Mark's fears was explained to Mark.

(ii)   The theory underlying graded exposure was explained to Mark.

(iii)  The difference between not being in control (of one's behaviour) and in control of one's behaviour was described and discussed.

(iv)   The theory underlying positive self-talk was explained to Mark.

(v)    Mark was taught slow deep breathing as a response to potential panic situations.

(vi)   Mark made a written agreement to 'become in control' and to carry out homeworks to achieve this (see Figure 6.12). Mark also agreed to keep a diary record of his homework tasks.

(vii)  Mark's diary record was reviewed with him on a weekly basis.

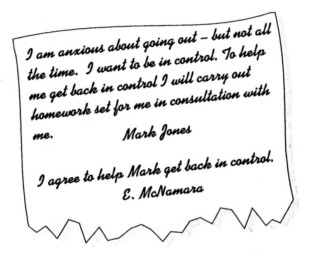

**Figure 6.12** Written agreement

*Outcome.* Over an 18 week period Mark progressively regained his confidence to go about the neighbourhood on his own or with friends. The progress was reflected in the contents of his diary (see Figures 6.13(a) and 6.13(b)).

It was indicated to Mark that he was now 'in control' and that there was now no need for him to continue to see the psychologist. A 'final challenge' was put to Mark: in the month or two after discharge, if he successfully coped in a situation similar to the two described earlier in which he had panicked, he was to write to the psychologist to inform him of the success. Three months after discharge the letter presented in Figure 6.14 was received. Naturally this was used to further consolidate Mark's success.

13th July 1997

Me and my mum went to Liverpool.

We went on the train and I went into the shop for my mum and she waited outside but I was very anxious about going in.

**Figure 6.13(a)** Diary entry at the beginning of the desensitisation programme

16th Nov. 1997

While I was watching Liverpool during the game I went down to get some food from the shop on my own. I wasn't anxious.

Me and my mum were in Ormskirk.

I went to one shop and she went to another and I met her in that shop. I wasn't anxious.

**Figure 6.13(b)** Diary entry towards the end of desensitisation programme (16 weeks later)

Dear Mr. McNamara,

I am writing to tell you that I've been Bowling with my friends. I went in February to Wigan bowling. It was John's birthday and his mum and dad took six of us and we went to play Quasar and Bowling. John's mum and dad left us for an hour. I wasn't frightened at all, I had a brilliant time.

I am still playing football for Brookside and Tranmere Rovers and I have just been told I have been kept on again for the 1998/1999 season.

I am playing for Tranmere in a tournament in Lancaster in the Easter holidays.

I have still been going to watch Liverpool when they play at home but they arn't playing well at the moment.

Thank you for helping me to get over my problem, I am ok with everything now when I'm left on my own and when I go out.

Yours sincerely,

Mark

**Figure 6.14** 'Challenge met' letter

## CASE STUDY 5 – PEER FEAR (BULLYING)

Andrew, a second year High School student, was reluctant to attend school. His parents reported that he appeared depressed at home and they consulted the school when he aired views such as 'Life's not worth living' and 'I'm going to kill myself'. The school referred Andrew to the Educational Psychologist.

In the *diagnostic interview* with Andrew and his mother it was reported that the difficulties had become apparent in the early part of the Autumn term. Clarification of the difficulties that Andrew was experiencing in school proved difficult as Andrew made sweeping generalisations about his situation – as the following abstract from the interview illustrates:

| | |
|---|---|
| *EP:* | Tell me more. |
| *Andrew:* | I'm going to kill myself. Life's not worth living. |
| *EP:* | Life's not worth living? |
| *Andrew:* | I'm getting battered at school. |
| *EP:* | When? |
| *Andrew:* | All the time. |
| *EP:* | Who by? |
| *Andrew:* | Everybody. |

*Formulation.* Andrew was anxious and depressed about school. The school situation was precipitating threats of self harm. Andrew's description of the factors precipitating his anxiety was too global to respond to at a specific level.

*First formulation.* Andrew's natural anxiety about the school situation was heightened by cognitive distortions, i.e. magnifications. Self evidently Andrew could not be being battered (physically assaulted) all the time by everybody.

*Intervention*

(i)   Andrew was asked to keep a diary record of incidents in school.
(ii)  Andrew's diary was reviewed weekly.

The intervention had a number of functions. First, the data gathered in Andrew's diary record could be used to test the hypothesis that Andrew's anxiety was contributed to by 'magnification'. Second, the diagnostic interview and consequent homework activity for Andrew indicated to Andrew that his situation was taken seriously and that something was being done about it.

*Evaluation.* The diary record revealed that:

(i)    On one day Andrew was hit twice by other pupils.
(ii)   Andrew was called names on about 50 per cent of the days he attended school.
(iii)  Eight different perpetrators of the bullying were identified.

*Outcome.* Reviewing the diary record with Andrew resulted in:

(i)    Andrew's assessment of the problem situation became more accurate.
(ii)   As a result of the above Andrew became less depressed and less anxious.
(iii)  The problem of bullying was successfully addressed by the school pastoral team.
(iv)   A three month follow up check with Andrew himself, his mother and teachers, revealed that the initial 'improvement' had been built upon and Andrew was attending school happily.

A fuller account of this case study is reported in McNamara 1998.

## CASE STUDY 6 – MIGRAINE INDUCED ANXIETY

Suzanne, aged 13 years, was referred to the Educational Psychologist by the GP. Suzanne had a history of suffering from migraine. Medication had been discontinued because of adverse side effects. After a bout of 'classical' migraine Suzanne could be unwell for a few days and not attend school.

The *diagnostic interview* with Suzanne and her mother revealed the following:

(i)     Suzanne's history of migraine went back a number of years.
(ii)    The migraine attacks were less frequent during school holidays.
(iii)   Although Suzanne experienced classical migraine attacks she also suffered lesser attacks which were headaches and nausea without the aura.
(iv)    Due to time away from school because of headaches the previous term, Suzanne had not completed one full week's attendance.
(v)     Suzanne worried about 'catching up' on school work after an absence.
(vi)    Suzanne's mother felt that the worry about school work contributed to further migraine attacks.

*Formulation.* The report that Suzanne experienced fewer headaches during the holidays was supportive of the view that missing school and the consequent disruption of continuity of school work contributed to the migraine attacks.

*Intervention*

(i)     Suzanne was taught progressive muscle relaxation and deep breathing and practised it each evening.
(ii)    Suzanne agreed to keep a record of her migraine attacks and to rate the severity (Figures 6.15(a) and 6.15(c)).
(iii)   Suzanne kept a record of the number of consecutive days that occurred that were headache free.
(iv)    Suzanne also kept a graph of her monthly 'headache score' (Figure 6.15(b)).
(v)     The results of Suzanne's self-monitoring were reviewed weekly for a term see 'Reviewing Skills' in Chapter 3).

*Outcome.* During the Autumn, out of the 14 week school term Suzanne attended eight of the weeks without any absences. Suzanne and her mother also reported that both the frequency and severity of the headaches had diminished.

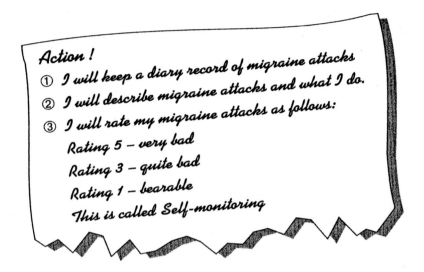

**Figure 6.15(a)** Recorded agreement with Suzanne

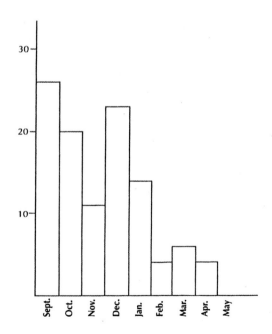

**Figure 6.15(b)** Graph of monthly headache score

# HEADACHE CHART – SEPTEMBER - JANUARY

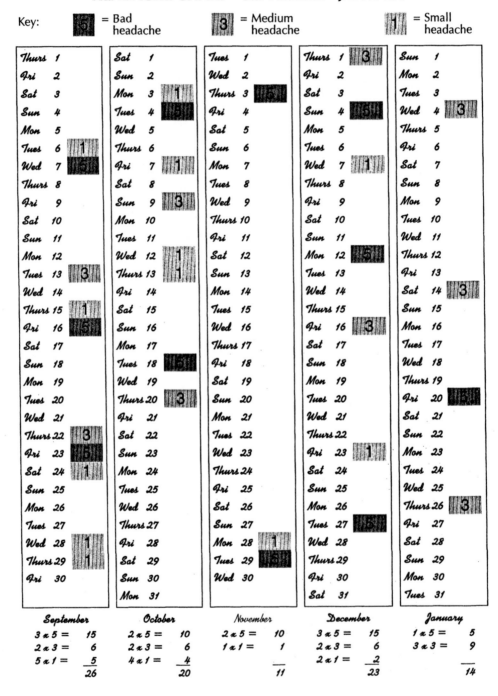

**Figure 6.15(c)**  Record and rating of headache occurrences

## CONCLUDING OBSERVATIONS

The incidence of anxiety states in children and adolescence is not known exactly but many authorities estimate it to be above 10 per cent. A proportion of these anxiety states will not require professional involvement but a significant proportion will. The number of mental health professionals with core skills in anxiety management, e.g. Clinical and Educational Psychologists, is such that there are insufficient numbers to cope with all the children and adolescents who might warrant their involvement. However, many of the milder anxiety problems can be dealt with by primary care workers, e.g. GPs, social workers, community nurses – without recourse to specialist psychologists and other mental health professionals.

Teachers too can be considered primary care workers to the extent that many of the anxiety problems experienced or manifest in the school setting will in the first instance be referred to members of the pastoral team (form tutors, Heads of Year). Teachers with a knowledge of the theory and practice of anxiety management can fulfil a preventative role; they are also in a good position to detect the early signs of anxiety and to respond in a manner which forestalls the precipitation of a full-blown anxiety state.

Finally, teachers with a knowledge of anxiety state theory and practice are in a position to work collaboratively with mental health professionals to respond to the more serious anxieties, fears and phobias that can and do occur in child and adolescent school populations.

# CHAPTER 7

# Tackling disaffection and apathy

The aims of this chapter are to:

(i) Consider the concept of 'motivation'.
(ii) Describe the 'stages of change' model.
(iii) Describe the aims of motivational interviewing.
(iv) Describe the techniques of motivational interviewing.
(v) Consider the use of questions (Socratic questioning).
(vi) Descibe the assessment of pupil motivation to change.

In the current educational climate everyone is encouraged to promote active pupil learning, empower pupils, engage in cooperative learning and develop non-coercive pupil management skills. These are admirable aims but to a large extent their achievement depends on a commitment from the pupils to share the aspirations and goals of their teachers. In other words, pupils have to feel motivated.

This chapter is concerned with strategies that can be used to elicit commitment to change from pupils, i.e. elicit intrinsic motivation. The counselling approach which incorporates these strategies is known as 'motivational interviewing'. If such commitment can be elicited, then internal regulation of behaviour can be fostered so that the teacher–learner interaction is one of cooperative learning, not imposed learning. While the emphasis of this chapter is on school-related problems, the description of the theory and practice of motivational interviewing has applicability to a wide range of counselling situations.

## MOTIVATION

Motivation is a very important concept because of its central role in facilitating pupil endeavour. Although the concept of motivation may appear elusive, at the practical level teachers and psychologists have addressed the many factors that influence pupil behaviour in order to facilitate pupil learning.

Covington (1992) identified three sources of motivation:

(i) emotion – feelings can arouse and inhibit action;
(ii) cognition – thoughts can trigger, sustain and inhibit action;
(iii) physiology – heightened levels of adrenalin can produce fight or flight responses.

These *internal* motivational factors contrast with the *external* motivational factors, usually rewards and sanctions, that are often incorporated into teachers' whole class and individual pupil management strategies.

Rewards and punishments can be considered aspects of motivation in that good behaviour tends to occur more frequently when it is rewarded and less frequently when it is punished. As rewards and punishments are environmental consequences of behaviour they are considered to be *external motivators*.

However, individuals may wish to behave in some ways but not in other ways regardless of external consequences. For example, on one occasion a student may wish to go to a discotheque and have 'a good time' and on another occasion the student may forego the visit to the discotheque in order to study – consequently not experiencing the 'good time'. In this latter situation the environmental determinant of behaviour (discotheque attendance and associated 'good time') is overridden by internal controls or *internal motivators*. Therefore at any given time behaviour is governed by the interaction of internal and external motivational factors. The *self regulation* of behaviour can be viewed as the degree of control an individual exercises over the environmental influences on behaviour.

In educational situations learning experiences are designed to facilitate student learning. Teachers attempt to make the experiences interesting so that the students will persist at the tasks in the face of difficulty, i.e. be motivated. This scenario constitutes an example of the teacher setting up a learning situation to elicit *internal motivation*.

In addition to making the learning activity interesting the teacher also gives the student feedback both during and after task completion. This feedback, when positive, is reinforcing and encourages the student to continue to apply themselves to academic task demands. Such teacher behaviour – praise, feedback and encouragement – constitutes *external motivation*.

Teachers may not always succeed in making the academic task demands interesting. Consequently external motivational systems are often developed to reward pupils, i.e. motivate them. These systems may include social reinforcement (praise and attention), stars, stickers, team points, certificates or free choice of activity.

External motivational systems are very effective in the Primary school sector and can also be effective in the Secondary school sector. However the use of 'crude' external motivational systems such as stars, stickers, house or team points is less age appropriate in the Secondary educational sector; to the extent that there is an expectation that as pupils grow older so they will become less reliant on external motivational systems and will become more self-motivating.

## SELF-MOTIVATION

The concept of self motivation is complex – for the internal self-regulatory system is influenced by many factors, e.g. aspirations and feelings of competency. Learning in a school context is not always pleasant and interesting. It usually requires a lot of effort and persistence from the learner. Some learning activities may even create discomfort and tension and therefore be resisted by the student. When there is resistance to learning the institution of an external motivational system has to overcome this resistance. Even when successful, this external regulation of behaviour is really only a temporary solution, for it is important that pupils learn to regulate their own behaviour and do not come to rely solely on external forms of regulation.

In summary, there are both internal and external regulatory systems that determine how students behave. The external regulatory system is made up of the environmental factors that influence behaviour. The internal regulatory system is more complex and is made up of such things as the student's aspirations and feelings of competency.

Motivation is not a unitary construct but is a term used to summarise the net effect of all the internal and external factors that influence behaviour.

## PUPIL MOTIVATION

Boekaerts (1994) has described three different levels at which motivation can be studied in educational situations. They are the *superordinate level*, the *middle level* and the *momentary level*.

*Superordinate level:* this refers to the student's general inclination towards learning.
*Middle level:* this refers to the student's inclination and attitude towards different areas of learning, e.g. science, languages or music.
*Momentary level:* This refers to the student's commitment to specific curricular tasks.

When students do not show an inclination towards learning at either the superordinate and middle levels and spasmodic or negligible inclination at the momentary level, they are variously described as *disaffected, disillusioned, alienated, passive* and *reluctant* learners. If such personal dispositions find expression in behaviours which unduly interfere with the learning and teaching processes in classroom situations the pupils are referred to as *disruptive*.

The above array of labels used to describe pupils communicates a negative outlook with respect to educational and social achievement. Firstly, the pupils do not share a commitment to the goals and aspirations of their educational institution and teachers. Secondly, inherent in these descriptions of the students is the assumption that the pupils concerned are not motivated to change and therefore their situation is permanent and unchangeable. This is a rather pessimistic scenario given the increasing concern about the growing numbers of disaffected pupils.

Fortunately pupil management techniques have been developed to effect change in pupil behaviour. These techniques are described in Chapters 2, 3 and 4 of this book and aim to bring the pupil behaviour under teacher control. This 'control state' is something of a halfway house for ideally the control state aimed for should be self-control, i.e. the pupil should be in control of and regulating his or her own learning. There can of course be degrees of self-control. This concept is best illustrated by viewing the locus of control as being somewhere along a continuum the poles of which are teacher control and pupil self-control. This concept is illustrated in Figure 7.1. The concept of a continuum allows for the proposition that pupil behaviour may be partially under teacher control (externally regulated), and partially under pupil self-control (internally regulated). *There can be degrees of self-control.*

The external regulation of pupil behaviour can be viewed as an external motivational system. However it may be the case that pupils do not wish to behave in pro-social and pro-academic ways, in which case this resistance has to be overcome when instituting an external motivational system has to overcome this resistance. Attempts to institute external motivational systems to address disaffection have usually focused on changing pupil behaviour, specifically at changing academic behaviour, but this may be too narrow a focus of intervention for disaffection is more than negative academically orientated behaviour.

**Figure 7.1** The continuum of control (Jolly and McNamara 1994)

## Disaffection

This consists of an integrated set of negative attitudes, beliefs and behaviours with respect to the demands of school life generally and to academic demands in particular.

Given these characteristics of disaffection it is difficult to identify, construct and implement an external pupil management programme that will achieve all the necessary change. This difficulty is becoming increasingly recognised and responded to.

## Tackling disaffection

Human activity takes place in three modalities – *thinking, feeling* and *behaving*. There is a relationship and a degree of interdependency between how people think, feel and behave and this relationship can be presented in diagrammatic form (see Figure 7.2).

This model illustrates why attempts to effect change in human behaviour solely through the modality of *behaviour* is unnecessarily restrictive – for it ignores the possibility of effecting change through the modalities of thinking and feeling. In addition, if the behavioural difficulties are a consequence of faulty thinking, then to address the behavioural difficulty without addressing the faulty thinking may be ineffective, i.e. if *dysfunctional thinking* results in *dysfunctional behaviour* then the dysfunctional thinking should be addressed.

## Self change

When an individual engages in inappropriate behaviour the movement to engaging in appropriate behaviour involves two stages. The *first stage* involves the individual deciding that they wants to change, i.e. they become motivated to

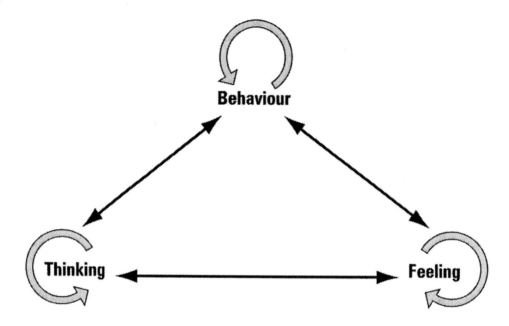

**Figure 7.2** The interactional relationship between thinking, feeling and behaving

change. The *second stage* involves translating the commitment into successful action: it is important to remember that wishing for change does not mean that it will be achieved for striving for change can be hampered by lack of the skills necessary to achieve the change.

Stage one is probably best achieved by counselling techniques, i.e. talking therapies. Stage two is more likely to be achieved by behavioural and/or cognitive behavioural strategies. Behavioural strategies have been described the earlier chapters. This chapter is concerned with stage one – strategies for eliciting commitment to change. The counselling approach that incorporates these strategies is known as motivational interviewing. If such commitment can be elicited then internal regulation of behaviour can be fostered so that the teacher–learner interaction is that of *cooperative learning*, not *imposed learning*.

## MOTIVATIONAL INTERVIEWING

This counselling approach enables counsellors, teachers and other professionals to address a lack of motivation to change in a structured and positive manner. Motivational interviewing has proved successful with clients presenting with addictive behaviours (e.g. to heroin, alcohol). By 'proved successful' is meant that clients who may have been coerced into treatment have become motivated and have actively committed themselves to the treatment programmes (Miller and Rollnick 1991).

In educational situations some pupils do not want to be in school and do not share the goals and aspirations of their teachers. By analogy, it seems appropriate to address the problems of these pupils using the counselling approach of motivational interviewing.

There is an extensive literature on the effectiveness of self-management programmes (e.g. Kanfer and Spates 1977). The use of any self-management programme is dependent on the commitment of the pupil to change his or her own behaviour. There must be commitment to both the behaviour change and to the self-change programme. Thus, eliciting pupil commitment to behaviour change is a necessary prerequisite for pupils to engage in self-management programmes. Lack of commitment to change is an obstacle to change particularly pertinent to the situations of the pupils who qualify for the various descriptors used previously to describe some pupils, i.e. alienated, reluctant, passive, poorly motivated, disaffected.

The counselling approach described as motivational interviewing *is* an effective way of eliciting pupil commitment to behaviour change – change that is necessary if the pupil is to access and implement self-management programmes. Apart from designated staff with significant pastoral responsibilities, it is unlikely that many teachers will engage in motivational interviewing in counselling situations – but most teachers with a knowledge of the theory and techniques of motivational interviewing can incorporate some of the techniques into their day to day conversations with pupils.

A description of motivational interviewing (MI) is presented in this section. The structure for this section is as follows:

The model of the *stages of change*
The *theory* and *goals* of MI – goals that facilitate movement from the stage in which the pupil does not accept that a problem exists (precontemplative) to the decision to change stage (determinism) in which the pupil has accepted that a problem exists and has decided to do something about it.
The *strategies and techniques* used in MI.

## The model of the stages of change

In 1982 Prochaska and DiClemente critically analysed over 150 psychotherapies. As a result of this analysis they identified two stages to the effective achievement of therapeutic change:

(i)   a commitment to change, and
(ii)  the achievement of the change.

The authors also described a general model of the stages of change – a model that is described as having six stages. This stages of change model (see Figure 7.3) is central to the practice of MI.

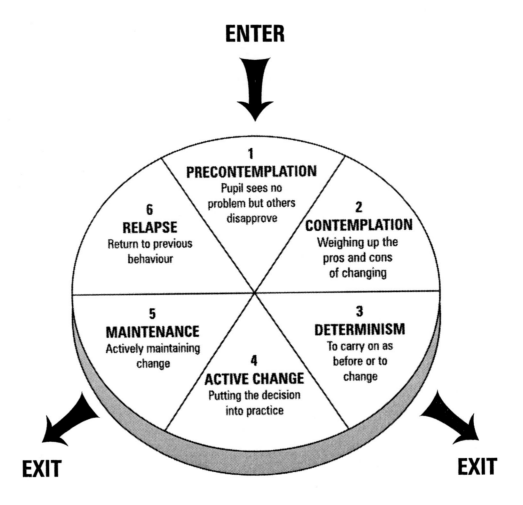

**Figure 7.3** The model of the stages of change

### *Stage 1 Precontemplative*

In this stage the client* does not acknowledge that a problem exists. The client may not be conscious or aware that a problem exists or may not accept that the situation is problematic. In this stage it is not the client who thinks that he or she has a problem, but rather significant others, e.g. parents, teachers, counsellors, society. The disaffected pupil is in the precontemplative phase. There are many reasons to be in precontemplation. Miller and Rollnick (1991) summarise these reasons under the headings

(i)   reluctance
(ii)  resignation
(iii) rationalisation
(iv)  rebellion.

*Reluctant precontemplators.* These are people who through lack of knowledge or inertia do not want to consider change. This phase is characterised by a lack of explicit awareness either about the *impact of the problem* or sometimes even an awareness of *the facts* about the problem. Reluctant precontemplators are characterised by a *reluctance to change* rather than a *resistance to change*. The counselling strategy to address reluctant contemplators aims to raise *knowledge, awareness* and *concern* about the problem.

*Resigned precontemplators.* These are people who appear to have given up on the possibility of change and who are resigned to the status quo. They sometimes feel overwhelmed by their problem(s) and either do not want to even think about it or feel that it is too late to do anything about it. They may well have tried unsuccessfully in the past to tackle the problem. The counselling strategy to address resigned precontemplators aims to both instill hope – by promoting feelings of *self-efficacy* and *internal attribution* – and to explore the barriers to change.

*Rationalising precontemplator.* These are people who can readily identify reasons why the problem is not a problem or why it may be a problem for other people but not for themselves. The rationalising precontemplator often feels that they have all the answers – in contrast to the resigned precontemplator who feels that they have none of the answers. The rationalising precontemplator can be differentiated from the rebellious precontemplator in that the resistance of the former is more in the *thinking* whereas the resistance of the latter is more in the *emotions*. Empathy and reflection are the counselling techniques of particular use, particularly double sided reflection: for example,

*Pupil:*    'I can work when I want to'.
*Teacher:*  'Sometimes you don't work'.

---

*When general statements about the use of MI are made the terms 'client' and 'counsellor' are used. When statements about the use of MI are made with reference to children and young people then the term 'pupil' or 'student' is used and the terms 'counsellor' and 'teacher' are used interchangeably.

*Rebellious precontemplators.* These are people who usually present as hostile and resistant to change. Rebellious precontemplators often exhibit low self-esteem incorporating external attributions and low feelings of self-efficacy.

### Observations on the precontemplative stage

(a) It may be particularly difficult to move a client on from the precontemplative stage. It is therefore important for the counsellor to have as the initial goal movement towards the comtemplative phase – and not to a decision to either change or not change – for if the contemplative phase is under emphasised the client may well decide on the status quo. However it must also be recognised that the client may wish to exercise informed choice and carry on for the present with what others consider a problematic behaviour. At the least the counsellor tries to ensure that this is an informed choice by eliciting and bringing into full consciousness (i) information about the behaviour, and (ii) the impact and consequences of the behaviour.

(b) 'The problem' may not mean the same thing to the client as it does for the counsellor. For example, a student may be referred to a school counsellor for persistently copying another student's homework. The student may see the problem as 'getting caught' rather than one of copying per se.

(c) We cannot *make* precontemplators change of their own free will – and it is usually counterproductive to try to do so. Rather, as noted by DiClemente (1981):

> It is particularly important to use **careful motivational strategies**, rather than to mount high-intensity programs or efforts that will be ignored by those uninterested in changing the particular problem behaviour.

DiClemente goes on to assert:

> It is just as false to believe that precontemplators don't ever change and there is nothing we can do. We cannot make precontemplators change but we **can motivate them to move to contemplation**.

### Stage 2 Contemplative

In this phase the client is willing to consider the problem and the possibility that change may be desirable and beneficial. Many clients with problems present themselves to the counsellor at the contemplative rather than the precontemplative stage for the contemplative stage is a stage of ambivalence. For example, many smokers do consider that smoking may be a problem but they do not give up smoking. What the counsellor has to facilitate is a move from the contemplative stage to the decision stage, i.e. determination to take action to give up smoking. Motivational interviewing strategies aim to assist in the movement to decision making. These strategies include eliciting information about (i) the negative consequences of the problem, and (ii) the positive consequences of change. Eliciting personal information from the client is far more powerful than the counsellor providing information at a more general level. It is important during the contemplative stage that the pros and cons of the *change* are considered as well as the pros and cons of the *problem behaviour.* For example, the problem behaviour may be disruptive classroom behaviour. The pros of this from the pupil's perspective may be that (i) the teachers focus on social behaviour and let poor quality academic behaviour go without comment, and (ii) the pupil may gain peer group esteem. The cons are that the pupil will (i) not do well academically (ii) be subject to disciplinary consequences, and (iii) have reports of unsatisfactory behaviour sent to parents.

The pros and cons of change could be as follows. The pros:

(i) academic progress is more likely;
(ii) sanctions will be avoided; and
(iii) parental approval will be forthcoming.

The cons might be:

(i) peer group ridicule for changing from oppositional to compliant behaviour; and
(ii) the perception that changing behaviour from oppositional to cooperative was synonymous with the teachers 'winning' and the self 'losing'.

### Observations on the contemplative stage

(a) It may be possible to anticipate some of the possible cons of changing and plan to minimise their effect. Sometimes the cons of change may have been identified because of previous unsuccessful attempts to change: for example

> *Pupil:* When I did my homework on Tuesday I had to miss training (football) and so they put me on the bench.
> *Teacher:* So you want to do your homework on Tuesday night but you also want to go to football training.

(b) Contemplation is not a commitment to change. This is an important distinction to make as failure to engage a client in a treatment programme may be a consequence of misinterpreting interest in changing (i.e. contemplation) with a decision to change. For example, during health campaigns in the workplace, it is not uncommon for between 70 per cent to 80 per cent of the smokers to express an interest in giving up smoking. When programmes are developed and offered the take up rate is often less than 5 per cent. This is strong empirical evidence that interest is not synonymous with commitment to change. The 'missing link' in such health promotional activities is a motivational strategy to facilitate a move from contemplation to determination and readiness to take action. In educational situations scenarios which reflect the above contemplation/decision to change 'missing link' are not uncommon. When pupils are referred to the form tutor because of misdemeanours it is not uncommon for the pupil to *agree to change* their behaviour but within days *be re-referred* for similar behaviour.

On this basis the pupil may be described as insincere, expedient, lacking self-control, or lacking appropriate social skills. Any of these conclusions may be accurate, but it may be that in the counselling situation the pastoral teacher either:

- concluded the interview when the pupil was in the contemplative stage and misinterpreted this as a decision to change on the part of the pupil; or
- concluded *for the pupil* that the pupil would change their behaviour.

The techniques of motivational interviewing, particularly that of *eliciting concern*, facilitate client movement from contemplation to decision to change (see 'M I–Advanced Techniques' later in this chapter).

(c) Sometimes the client will have made previous unsuccessful attempts to change their behaviour, i.e. overcome the problem(s). Analysis of these attempts can:

  - help identify obstacles to effective change; and
  - identify 'limited success' – and build on this – using the technique of positive restructuring, (see 'MI – Advanced Techniques') to promote feelings of self-efficacy and hence the probability of commitment to change.

### Stage 3 Determinism – commitment to action

This stage is characterised by the decision to take action to cease engaging in problematic behaviour and/or engage in positive behaviour. *The client appears ready for and committed to action.* This stage, while characterised by the decision to take action, also includes preparing and planning for change.

When a client is identified to be in the determination phase it is important not to conclude that this is a stable state – for there exists the possibility that the client may revert to the contemplative phase, it is usually the case that all ambivalence has not been fully resolved. During the 'planning for change' activities it is important to respond to all the opportunities available to consolidate the move from precontemplation, through contemplation, to determinism (i.e. to reflect back the client utterances indicative of increased knowledge, concern, internal attribution and selfefficacy.

The planning stage involves:

(i)    deciding what the client will actually do; and
(ii)   identifying possible pitfalls and obstacles, and appropriate responses to them.

Commitment and enthusiasm for change cannot make up for lack of skills. Therefore the planning strategy to address both (i) and (ii) involves problem solving strategies, i.e. eliciting from the client possible responses and facilitating wise choices. It should always be remembered that strong commitment alone does not guarantee change.

### Stage 4 Active change – implementing the plan

The plan to achieve change is implemented by the client between the end of the session at which the plan was agreed and the beginning of the first session of the action phase. The action phase sessions serve a variety of purposes for the pupil. The purposes are to provide:

(i)    an opportunity to make *a public commitment* to change;
(ii)   an opportunity to receive *confirmation and support* for the plan;

(iii)   an opportunity to receive *external feedback* on progress of the plan;

(iv)   an opportunity to receive *positive reinforcement* for programme success.

(v)   an opportunity to receive *positive feedback* after verbalising feelings and thoughts of self-efficacy and internal attributions;

(vi)   as a result of (v) increase in sense of self-efficacy and internal attribution.

### Stage 5 Maintenance

The length of time that the client is involved in the action stage is variable. During the action stage the new pattern of behaviour is built up and consolidated. In the maintenance phase the specific active support of the counsellor and of the programme strategies – e.g. graphing of record of successful behaviour change – is withdrawn. In a sense the maintenance phase is a 'test' of the success of the intervention programme; for, ideally, the behaviour change achieved by the intervention will carry on when the programme is phased out.

### Stage 6 Relapse

This phase completes the stages of change model. In a sense it can be considered a stage that gives added validity to the model in that it reflects the reality that even when change is achieved and sustained there always exists the possibility that relapse may occur.

A knowledge of the stages of change model facilitates the counsellor supporting the client to re-enter the cycle at the appropriate stage. If the relapse is recognised and referred to the counsellor early enough, then the re-entry may be at the action phase; if referral is delayed, the re-entry may be at the contemplative phase.

A major strength of the model is the inclusion of the relapse phase since this is an explicit recognition that clients may relapse: it constitutes a positive and optimistic message that relapse should not be interpreted as 'the problem cannot be overcome' but the that 'sometimes a tough problem is not completely overcome at the first attempt'.

### The goals of motivational interviewing

There are five specific goals of motivational interviewing: they are to:

increase *knowledge*
increase *concern*
promote *self-efficacy*
promote *internal attribution*
promote *self-esteem*.

The first two of the goals are directed at facilitating client movement from the precontemplative stage to the contemplative stage: the second two are directed at facilitating client movement from the contemplative stage to the determination stage, i.e. to a position where the client decides to change.

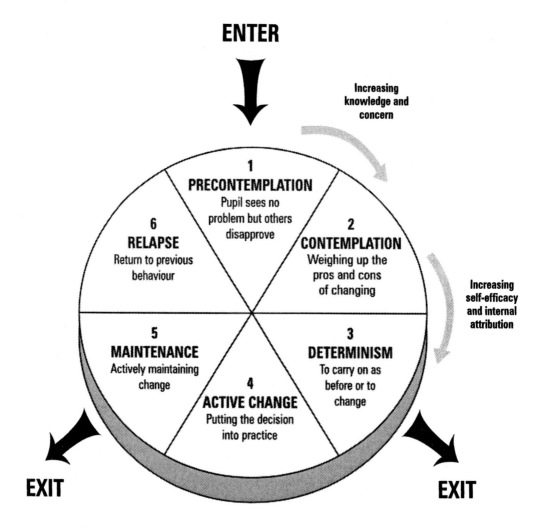

**Figure 7.4** Facilitating movement through the atates of change

The first two goals are to promote *knowledge* of the problem situation and *concern about* the problem situation. If these two goals are achieved then client movement is facilitated away from the precontemplative stage and towards the contemplative stage. In parallel with these two goals are the aims of promoting client feelings and beliefs of *self-efficacy* and an *internal attribution* of 'the causes' of the problem.

In the counselling situation these objectives are not striven for in a sequential linear fashion, i.e. first elicit knowledge about the problem situation, then elicit concern, then promote feelings of an internal attributional disposition and self-efficacy. The counselling situation is dynamic and interactive: the skill of the counsellor lies in identifying opportunities to move towards the goals and respond to them effectively using the strategies of MI.

The four goals of MI described above are of particular importance as their relationship to client movement within the model of the stages of change is central to the practice of MI (see Figure 7.4).

There is a fifth goal of MI – *promoting self-esteem*. Everybody has a picture of themselves, their self-image. People can evaluate their self-image positively or negatively. If people self-evaluate themselves positively they are said to have high self-esteem, whereas if they self-evaluate negatively they are said to have low self-esteem. This is perhaps an oversimplistic notion of self-esteem, for people's evaluation of themselves can vary according to the frame of reference used. For example, a pupil may have low self-esteem in the academic domain, evaluating themselves as academically less able; whereas in the sporting domain the same pupil may evaluate themselves as a high achiever. High self-esteem facilitates movement both from the precontemplative stage to the contemplative stage and from the contemplative stage to the determination (decision to change) stage.

If a client is low in self-esteem then the likelihood that they will *generate* and *accept negative information* about their situation is reduced; for to accept such negative feedback might further diminish their self-esteem. However a client with high self-esteem will be more likely to accept and respond constructively to negative feedback. The client low in self-esteem is therefore less likely to accept negative feedback and more likely to engage in *denial or projection*: projection, a tendency to blame others or attribute the cause of the problem to external factors, is particularly obstructive to client movement through the stages of change as it is indicative of an external attribution style, i.e. the client's analysis of the problem can be reduced to the proposition:

> the causes of the problem are other people and/or environmental factors: therefore it's not my problem . . . and in any event there's nothing I can do about it.

The techniques of MI aim to help the client move away from this position to one in which the client acknowledges a problem, decides to do something about it and feels that he or she can succeed with the chosen strategy.

The objectives and rationale of MI are summarised in Figure 7.5.

If a pupil is entered on the special needs register of a school then he or she is entitled to an Individual Educational Programme (IEP). When the IEP targets the behaviour of a pupil it is often referred to as an Individual Behaviour Plan (IBP). The IBP has maximum chance of success if the pupil (i) agrees the need for it, and (ii) commits themselves to it. This proposition is illustrated in Figure 7.6.

## Motivational interviewing techniques

The techniques of MI can be considered an amalgam of humanistic, Rogerian and behavioural counselling.

The *humanistic* component is an unconditional positive regard for the client: value judgements about the client as a person are not made.

The *Rogerian* component takes the form of non-directive counselling. The Rogerian method in its pure form takes the form of totally non directive counselling, i.e. the counsellor follows the direction of the client. By reflecting back to the client the client's own utterances the counsellor uses the client's statements, observations and feelings to elicit further statements, observations and feelings. Thus the counsellor joins the client on the client's 'journey'.

| CONCEPT | OBJECTIVE | REASON |
|---|---|---|
| Knowledge | Promote | Increase the probability of movement from the precontemplative to contemplative stage |
| Concern | Promote | Increase the probability of movement from the precontemplative to contemplative stage **and** thence to determination, i.e. a decision to change |
| Self-esteem | Promote | Negative feedback will be more readily accepted and likelihood of denial, rejection and projection reduced |
| Internal Attribution | Promote | i) Increases belief that causes of 'the problem' can be influenced and<br>ii) increases the probability that 'failure' will be attributed to lack of effort not to external factors |
| Self-Efficacy | Promote | Facilitates the belief that change is achievable and increases<br>i) persistence when the task proves difficult and<br>ii) continued commitment when initial efforts result in failure |

**Figure 7.5** Within person variables: therapeutic objectives and rationale to elicit/facilitate client motivation

The *behavioural* component of MI is used to modify the Rogerian component so that the *non-directive* approach becomes a *guided* approach. This is achieved by the use of *selective active listening*. Before describing the characteristics of selective active listening, active listening – a core component of most counselling approaches – is described.

### Active listening

Active listening has both non-verbal and verbal dimensions. Active listening involves communicating to the client that what he or she says is of interest, relevance, importance and worth listening to – it is valued.

The *non-verbal* behaviours that communicate this value include eye contact, facial expression and posture. For example, if the counsellor sits back, arms

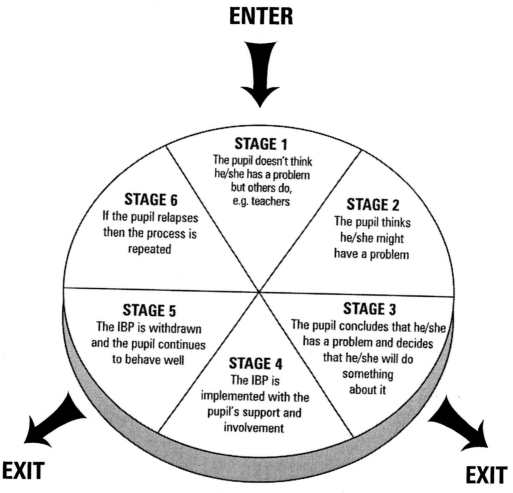

**ENTER**

**STAGE 1**
The pupil doesn't think
he/she has a problem
but others do,
e.g. teachers

**STAGE 2**
The pupil thinks
he/she might
have a problem

**STAGE 6**
If the pupil relapses
then the process is
repeated

**STAGE 3**
The pupil concludes that he/she
has a problem and decides
that he/she will do
something
about it

**STAGE 5**
The IBP is withdrawn
and the pupil continues
to behave well

**STAGE 4**
The IBP is
implemented with the
pupil's support and
involvement

**EXIT**

**EXIT**

**Figure 7.6** Individual Behaviour Plans and the stages of change

folded and intermittently looks at the clock on the office wall, this would not constitute active listening: active listening would include eye contact, leaning towards the client and nodding to give the client non-verbal feedback demonstrating that the therapist is following, understanding and sympathetic to what the client is saying.

The *verbal* manifestations of active listening include *reflecting, summarising* and *structuring* the client's utterances.

### Reflecting

This can consist of parroting/repeating, rewording and paraphrasing.

*Parroting/repeating.* This involves simply repeating the exact words used by the client:

*Pupil:*     'I nearly always do my homework'.
*Counsellor:*  'You nearly always do your homework'.

It is important that this reflection is not received by the client as a question: for the client may then respond with a 'yes' or a 'no' consequently closing down rather than opening up the exploration of a problem area. The counsellor guards against allowing a reflection slipping into becoming a question by slightly lowering, rather than making slightly higher, the tone of voice at the end of the reflection. This technique should not be overused as this may irritate the client.

At this point the counsellor might be tempted to ask *direct questions* to elicit information: e.g. about the specifics of homework completion and non-completion:

> tell me the homework you get each night and tell me which homeworks you usually do and those you don't?

This temptation should be resisted. The time to ask direct questions is at the determination stage, i.e. after the client has made a decision to change; the client can then be asked direct questions as part of the collaborative procedure to agree a self-change programme. The use of selective active listening is the strategy used at this early stage to elicit further information and some concern about the problem (see 'Examples of selective active listening' later in this chapter).

At this early point in the counselling process direct questions should be kept to a minimum. Direct questions may

– allow the client to reply 'yes' or a 'no' and consequently close down the area of enquiry;
– elicit resistance from the client as personal disclosures at an early stage of the procedure may be threatening to the client and not supportive of moves towards the four key objectives of motivational interviewing.

*Rewording.* This involves restating the client's utterances, using different words and synonyms. This is particularly useful when the client uses colloquial terms:

*Pupil:*     I threw a rubber at the teacher and it hit him on the side of the head . . . it was wicked.
*Teacher:*   You hit the teacher on the head with a rubber and you now realise that it was a bad thing to do. (i.e. a statement, not a question).
*Pupil:*     No . . . it was great . . . it was a good laugh . . . everyone was laughing their heads off.

In this case the pupil was not using the dictionary meaning of the word 'wicked' but a colloquial meaning indicating enjoyable and amusing. This is the main purpose of using rewording – for it helps to establish that the client and counsellor both mean/understand the same things by the words used. The use of rewording also avoids the potential of irritating the client by the use of parroting.

*Paraphrasing.* This counsellor's reflective response moves away a little from merely attempting to reflect back *exactly* what is said (parroting) and establishing agreement about the *content* of what is said (rewording). The counsellor attempts to establish the *intention* and *underlying meaning* of the client's words. In a sense it can be seen as a hypothesis testing reflective response:

*Pupil:*     Everyone knows I'm hard.
*Teacher:*   You think that the other pupils see you as the toughest pupil in this school.
*Pupil:*     Yeah! They're all scared of me, the teachers too.

### Summarising

This strategy consists of the counsellor drawing together utterances of the client into a neat, succinct summary: this summary serves to allow the client to agree, disagree, modify or correct the counsellor's accuracy of summary. For example, after five or six client–counsellor interactions the counsellor might summarise as follows.

*Teacher:*    As I understand it, you have been excluded from school on three occasions. If you are excluded again it will be a permanent exclusion. At first, when I asked you how you felt about this, you said: 'I'm not arsed'. Now you said you are worried about it because it is unlikely that you will get a place in another school.

*Pupil:*       Yes.

A summary can be used by the counsellor as a stimulus to elicit further *information, concern* and possibly *commitment* to action from the client:

*Teacher:*    Not following teacher's instructions in class and then arguing with the teacher when asked to leave the classroom has led to you being excluded three times and the next exclusion may be permanent . . . and you do not want to be permanently excluded . . . what conclusion do you draw from this?

*Pupil:*       I suppose I'd better make sure I don't get into an argument with the teacher again.

### Structuring

Frequently in a counselling situation the client responds to the counsellor's prompts with information that can provide the counsellor with opportunities to further help the client volunteer more information about their situation. This in turn may provide the counsellor with opportunities to promote the development of client concern about their situation. However, information that has the potential, when reflected back, to promote concern in the client, might need structuring to enhance its potential to do this. For example:

*Teacher:*    Tell me more.
*Pupil:*       I'm not going to apologise to that dickhead.
*Teacher:*    You are not going to apologise to the head teacher.
*Pupil:*       No, even if I'm out of school for another two weeks.
*Teacher:*    You're not concerned about missing school.(*)
*Pupil:*       My GCSE exams start in three weeks and he's [the head teacher] not letting me back in for revision lessons.
*Teacher:*    You're worried about missing your revision lessons.(*)
*Pupil:*       Yes . . . you need five C-level GCSEs to get into the Sixth Form College.
*Teacher:*    Let's see if I've got it right. You want to go to the Sixth Form College and you need at least five C-level GCSEs to get there. If you don't resolve your difficulty with the headmaster you will be unable to attend revision lessons. If you don't go to revision lessons there's less chance of you getting five C-level GCSEs.
*Pupil:*       Yes.
*Teacher:*    What conclusion do you draw from my summary of what you've said?
*Pupil:*       'I don't know really . . . well I suppose I'd better try and get back into school for the revision lessons.

## Selective active listening

The behavioural component of MI is the crucial strategy used to facilitate client movement from the precontemplative stage, through the contemplative stage to the determination (decision to change) stage. The phrase 'active listening' is prefaced by the descriptor 'selective' because the counsellor *selectively* reflects back to the client that content of the client's verbalisations which facilitates the primary goals of MI being achieved, i.e. verbalisations that are indicative of

- specific information about the problem being made explicit
- concern about the problem being expressed
- feelings of enhanced self-efficacy
- indications of internal attribution.

### *Examples of selective active listening*

(a) Specific information about the problem being made explicit thus enhancing the client's knowledge.

> *Pupil:*      Michael's always messing around, that's why I hit him.
> *Teacher:*   You hit Michael.
> *Pupil:*      He's always getting on my nerves so I punched him.
> *Teacher:*   You punched Michael.
> *Pupil:*      Yes, and now I'm suspended.

The teacher only reflected back to the pupil those parts of the pupil's utterances that were leading to the nature of the pupil's unacceptable behaviour being made explicit. Consequently the parts of the utterances that did not facilitate this were ignored, i.e. 'Michael's always messing around . . .' and 'He's always getting on my nerves'. Thus, by being selective in what was reflected back to the pupil, the teacher elicited the nature of the problem behaviour from the pupil.

(b) Concern about the problem being elicited.

> *Pupil:*      Yes, and now I'm suspended.
> *Teacher:*   You punched Michael and as a result you have been suspended.
> *Pupil:*      Yes, I shouldn't have lost my temper.
> *Teacher:*   You lost your temper.
> *Pupil:*      I try to control it but sometimes I can't.
> *Teacher:*   Sometimes you can't control your temper.
> *Pupil:*      Yes, that's what gets me into trouble.

In this continuation of the MI interview the client is led from a description of a specific incident (punching Michael) to

(i)     the identification of a more general problem, losing his temper; and to
(ii)    an expression of concern about this general problem.

The technique of selective active listening is seen in the teacher reflecting back 'You lost your temper' but not 'I shouldn't have' and reflecting back 'Sometimes you can't control your temper' but not 'I try to control it'.

---

*This is an example of an advance technique, the reflection of concern, which is described later in this chapter

(c) Feelings of enhanced self-efficacy being promoted.

*Pupil:*      I've always done awful in all my exams except for science.
*Teacher:*   You've done well in science.
*Pupil:*      Only because I like science and I revised.
*Teacher:*   So when you revise you can do well in exams.

The teacher's first response, 'You've done well in science', is a selective reflection which emphasises a positive pupil achievement and therefore promotes feelings of self-efficacy: 'I've always done awful in exams', the negative component of the pupil's utterance, is ignored.

(d) Promoting an internal attribution bias. The above teacher–pupil interaction continued as follows:

*Pupil:*      Only because I like science and I revised.
*Teacher:*   So when you revise you can do well in exams.

The teacher's second response, 'when you revise you can do well in exams' is a selective reflection that supports the development of an internal attributional style.

## The techniques of motivational interviewing – a summary

Rogerian counselling is non-directive: the counsellor 'follows' the client's thoughts and feelings by reflecting back to the client the client's own verbalisations – which act as the eliciting stimuli or triggers for further client verbalisations, which, in turn, further develop the previous thoughts and feelings.

In contrast to Rogerian counselling, behavioural counselling is directive: the counsellor selectively reflects back to the client. The reflections emphasise the contents of the client's verbalisations which are most likely to act as eliciting stimuli or triggers to lead or guide the client to further develop their verbalisations about their behaviour, thoughts and feelings in a direction which results in increased knowledge (information) and concern, promotes self-esteem and enhances feelings of self-efficacy and an internal attributional tendency. Conversely, the counsellor either plays down or completely ignores the contents of the client's utterances that do not promote these aims of motivational interviewing. This is therefore a behavioural counselling strategy as the counsellor is *reinforcing* client utterances consistent with the goals of MI and *extinguishing* client utterances that are obstructive to these goals.

Motivational interviewing can be viewed as a synthesis of Rogerian and behavioural counselling to the extent that *non-directive strategies* are used to elicit a range of client utterances and these utterances are then responded to using *behavioural counselling strategies* to facilitate the client moving in the direction of the goals of MI.

## Motivational interviewing – advanced techniques

The four main advanced techniques are:

(i)     positive restructuring
(ii)    special reflections

(iii)   provoking
(iv)   Columbo technique.

### Positive restructuring

This involves feeding back with a positive interpretation, information given by the client with a negative interpretation:

> *Pupil:*     I missed four homeworks last week.
> *Teacher:*   You did six homeworks last week.

The aim of positive restructuring is to encourage a more positive self-image on the part of the pupil and to promote feelings of self-efficacy. Positive restructuring also strengthens the teacher–pupil relationship.

### Special reflections

At the simple level, reflections take the form of repeating, rewording or paraphrasing the client's statements. The aims are:

(i)    to ensure that the therapist understands what the client is saying and to communicate this to the client; and
(ii)   to elicit self-motivational statements.

Special reflections are extensions of simple reflections: there are four types.

(i)    reflection of feelings
(ii)   reflections of conflict
(iii)  overshooting
(iv)   undershooting.

*Reflections of feelings.* In this technique the counsellor attempts to reflect the feelings underlying the client's spoken words: it is to a degree a hypothesis testing approach for the counsellor has to make judgements about the client's feelings from his or her demeanour and tone of voice:

> *Pupil:*     I went to all my lessons except Mr Smith's.
> *Teacher:*   You don't like Mr Smith . . . or Chemistry.
> *Pupil:*     I used to like Chemistry but I hate Mr Smith.
> *Teacher:*   You hate Mr Smith.

Accurate feeling reflections can both develop and consolidate client–therapist rapport and elicit further 'feeling statements' from the client.

*Reflections of conflict.* The reflection of conflict is important as it indicates that the client is in the contemplative stage – a necessary prerequisite for a client's decision to change:

> *Pupil:*     I know I won't get to college if I don't pass my exams, but if I work my mates will take the piss out of me.
> *Teacher:*   You really want to work but you are worried about what your friends will say.

The aim of reflecting conflict is to elicit from the client a consideration of the pros and cons of changing, i.e. to consolidate the contemplative stage and then facilitate a move to the determination stage.

*Overshooting*. With this type of reflection the counsellor reflects a client's statement but exaggerates it:

| | |
|---|---|
| *Pupil:* | I don't like English, French, Maths, Science or RE. |
| *Teacher:* | You don't like any subjects. |
| *Pupil:* | Oh yes, I do, I like . . . |

The aim of overshooting is to elicit from the client confirmation of the 'overshoot', positive restructuring, qualification, modification or any other observation that 'refines' the client's response.

*Undershooting*. This is the opposite to overshooting. The counsellor reflects the client's utterances but plays down the contents:

| | |
|---|---|
| *Pupil:* | I can't stand some lessons. |
| *Teacher:* | You're not keen on some lessons. |
| *Pupil:* | I f***ing hate chemistry and physics. |

The aims of undershooting are to elicit an expression of intensity of feeling about aspects of the problem and to elicit specificity of feeling.

### Provoking

With this technique the counsellor reflects to the client that the client has no problems. The aim is to elicit from the client that he or she actually does have problems:

| | |
|---|---|
| *Teacher:* | You seem to be saying that you don't have a problem. |
| *Pupil:* | Well I wouldn't say that. |
| *Teacher:* | You do have a problem. |
| *Pupil:* | I suppose I could behave better in class. |
| *Teacher:* | You misbehave in class. |
| *Pupil:* | Only really in French and Music. |

Provoking can be considered an extreme form of undershooting.

### Columbo technique

Some clients feel threatened in the counsellor–client situation as they like to be in control: they resist what they perceive to be a counsellor dominant, client submissive relationship. This perception can sometimes be utilised to good effect. The counsellor feigns incompetence and thereby is not seen by the client as a threat. In fact the counsellor's 'inadequacy' may elicit a 'helping' response from the client:

| | |
|---|---|
| *Teacher:* | I know I'm supposed to know how to help you but I'm not sure I know what to suggest. |

*Pupil:*    Well John Smith's been using one of those self-assessment diaries and he hasn't been in trouble for ages.

Dr Henk Van Bilsen (1991) named this technique after the television series detective Columbo (played by actor Peter Falk). The Columbo technique can be a powerful facilitator of movement from the precontemplative stage to the contemplative stage and then to the determination stage.

Examples 1 and 2 are of increasing knowledge and concern leading to movement from the precontemplative stage to the contemplative stage with the opportunity to further progress to the determination stage.

### Example 1

*Pupil:*    I nearly always do my homework . . .

*Teacher:*  Nearly always . . . (a **reflection** that elicits the specific **information** that sometimes the pupil did not do his or her homework.

*Pupil:*    Well sometimes I don't.

*Teacher:*  Sometimes you don't do your homework . . . (a **reflection** that elicits further **detailed information** about non completion of homework.

*Pupil:*    Well, on Tuesday I have football and I'm pushed for time . . .

*Teacher:*  On Tuesday you usually don't do your homework because you go to football practice . . . (**summarising**, which elicits an **expression of concern**)

*Pupil:*    Yes, it's a pain.

*Teacher:*  It's a pain . . . (a **reflection of concern** which elicits further **information** – information about the negative consequences of non completion of homework)

*Pupil:*    Yes, I usually get lines or a detention.

*Teacher:*  You get lines or detention because you don't do your homework and you don't do your homework because you go to football practice . . . how do you feel about that? . . . (**summarising** followed by a **Socratic question** (see next section of chapter); this elicited **concern** and an observation indicating **lack of feelings of self-efficacy**)

*Pupil:*    I don't like it . . . but there's nothing I can do about it.

*Teacher:*  You want to do something about not doing your homework on Tuesday night? . . . (reflecting a *conflict* and eliciting reiteration of **feelings of lack of self-efficacy**)

*Pupil:*    Yes, but I can't.

*Teacher:*  Would you like to explore with me if there's anything you can do that you haven't thought of? . . . (a **question** aimed at eliciting a response indicating that the pupil is in the **contemplative stage** with an 'open door' to the **determination stage**)

Pupil:      'Yes'.

### Example 2

*Pupil:*    I got a 'U' an unclassified for Maths

*Teacher:*  You got an unclassified for Maths . . . (a **reflection** that elicits a response indicating feelings of **low self-efficacy** and **internal attribution**)

*Pupil:*     'Yes, I'm stupid. . .I didn't work hard or revise.

*Teacher:*     You didn't work hard or revise . . . (**selective active listening** – reflecting the internal attribution content; but the pupil focuses on external factors

*Pupil:*     No, I was knocking around with my mates . . . they've left school.

*Teacher:*     You were spending time with your friends . . . (**selective active listening** – reflecting the aspect of the pupil's utterance that was incompatible with spending time revising; this reflection elicited an indication of **conflict**)

*Pupil:*     Yes, and they take the piss out of me if I say I'm staying in to revise.

*Teacher:*     You wanted to stay in and revise but you didn't because your friends would make fun of you . . . (a **summary of the conflict** makes it explicit and elicits a positive conflict resolution statement from the pupil, i.e. movement – the **determination stage**)

*Pupil:*     Yes, I'm going to take no notice of them in the future.

*Teacher:*     Have you got a plan of what you will do? . . . (a question aimed at facilitating movement from the **determination stage** to the **active change stage**)

*Pupil:*     I'm not sure.

*Teacher:*     Would you like some help? . . . (a question eliciting confirmation that the pupil has moved to the **active change stage**)

*Pupil:*     Yes.

## Example 3

This example shows that eliciting concern and promoting feelings of self-efficacy and internal attribution facilitates movement from the precontemplation stage to the determination stage.

*Pupil:*     I hardly did any of my homeworks last week.

*Teacher:*     You did some homework last week . . . (**positive restructuring** – which promotes a positive self-image (**higher self-esteem**) and encourages feelings of **self-efficacy**: **specific information** is also elicited)

*Pupil:*     Yes . . . English and er, er Geography.

*Teacher:*     You didn't get into trouble with the English and Geography teachers . . . (**summarising** and **structuring** elicits pupil concern about getting into trouble for not completing homework)

*Pupil:*     No, thank goodness.

*Teacher:*     You don't like getting into trouble for not doing homeworks. You did your English and Geography homeworks and so didn't get into trouble with the English and Geography teachers. (further **summarising** and **structuring** incorporating the concern elicited creates the opportunity to ask a Socratic question which facilitates movement from the **contemplative stage** towards the **determination stage**)

What conclusion do you draw from that?

*Pupil:*    I should do all my homeworks because if I do I won't get into trouble.

*Teacher:*  Would you like me to show you some homework time management programmes? . . . (a **direct question** seeking confirmation that the pupil is at the **determination stage** and is ready to prepare to enter the **active change** stage)

*Pupil:*    Yes.

The examples illustrate that potentially the client can 'travel' in many different directions: the counsellor's role is to guide/facilitate the client travelling in directions which increase knowledge and concern and feelings of self-efficacy and an internal attributional style. In doing so the counsellor is facilitating movement from the precontemplative stage, through the contemplative and determination stages, to the active change stage.

## THE USE OF QUESTIONS

The basic strategy of motivational interviewing is the use of active listening and selective active listening techniques. Newcomers to counselling often express surprise that direct questioning is not a part of active listening: in addition, newcomers experience initial difficulty in not asking direct questions when engaging with clients.

Direct questioning is not a part of active listening because the purpose of active listening is to facilitate the client discovering, analysing and clarifying problems and going on to formulate personal responses. Direct questioning is obstructive to this process. For example, if the counsellor asks a direct question and the client answers 'yes' or 'no', the response can 'close down' the client's exploration of his or her situation. In addition if the counsellor asks questions relevant to a problem perceived by others but not the client, the client's resistance to the possibility that a problem exists might be consolidated:

### Example 1

*Pupil:*    I'm excluded [from school] and it's not fair.
*Teacher:*  How many times have you been excluded from school?
*Pupil:*    Three, and I still think it's not fair.

This limited client response can be compared with the more productive progress made by the client when the counsellor used reflective techniques rather than a direct question:

### Example 2

*Pupil:*    I'm excluded [from school] and it's not fair.
*Teacher:*  You're excluded!
*Pupil:*    Yes, once more and it's permanent.
*Teacher:*  Permanent!
*Pupil:*    Yes, if you get three exclusions you can't come back.

| Teacher: | How does that make you feel? (Socratic question) |
|---|---|
| Pupil: | Worried. |
| Teacher: | You're worried that if you get excluded from school once more the exclusion will be permanent. |
| Pupil: | Yes, I won't be able to get into another school so I won't be able to take my GCSEs. |

The direct question posed in Example 1 elicited the information desired but also provided the pupil with the opportunity to consolidate resistance to change and deny the problem. In contrast, the reflective listening strategy described in Example 2 elicited the same information as the direct question in Example 1 but also created the opportunity for pupil concern to be elicited – a necessary prerequisite for moving to the contemplative and determination stages.

## Socratic questioning

Re-examination of the counsellor's role in Example 2 reveals that a question was asked, namely 'How does that make you feel?' This was not a question which could elicit a response that could 'close down' the interview but an open-ended Socratic question. Socratic questioning is used to a degree during MI to facilitate 'guided discovery', i.e. to facilitate the client 'discovering' and verbalising concerns about his or her situation. While Socratic questioning should be used sparingly, it can nonetheless be a powerful facilitator of movement from the precontemplative stage to the contemplative stage and then to the determination stage. Its main advantages are that it:

(i) draws the client's *attention* to information and/or feelings which are relevant to the 'problem' situation but which are outside the client's current focus;

(ii) facilitates the client using the 'new' information or 'discovered' feelings to either *re-evaluate* a previous conclusion or *construct a new idea*;

(iii) tends to move the client from the *concrete to the more abstract*;

(iv) formulates the question so that the client is *able to respond.*

Examples of these four characteristics of Socratic questioning are to be found in Example 2 above:

(i) Direct attention to feelings: 'How does that make you feel?'

(ii) Discover feelings: 'Worried.'

(iii) Moves from concrete to more abstract: *pupil moves on from fact of suspension to consequence/implication of suspension.*

(iv) Formulates the question so that pupil is able to answer: in Example 2 the pupil was able to answer the question 'How does that make you feel?' However in some circumstances it may be inappropriate to ask this question as the client may be unaware of their emotions. For example, if the pupil is offering information about their father who had deserted the family, they might not be able to respond to the question 'How does that make you feel?', but the pupil might be able to respond to the question 'Are you aware of any tension or discomfort when we talk about your father?'

Motivational interviewing is a collaborative endeavour and it breaches collaboration to ask questions that the client is unable to answer.

## ASSESSMENT OF PUPIL MOTIVATION TO CHANGE

The pupil's motivation to change can be assessed during the pupil interview/counselling session on the basis of the pupil's statements about the 'problem situation'. Undue weight should not be put on a single pupil statement. It should also be remembered that a pupil may be at different stages of the change model for different behaviours and that the pupil's assessment of his or her situation may vary at different moments or during different interview sessions, i.e. the pupil may be at the contemplative stage. Bearing these two provisos in mind, a number of pupil statements are listed below with an indication of where in the model of stages of change the pupil might be located.

| Pupil statement | Stage of change | Comment |
| --- | --- | --- |
| 1. I didn't swear at teacher. | Precontemplation | Disagrees with feedback of own behaviour (denial). |
| 2. I'm not disruptive. | Precontemplation | Disagrees with teacher's 'diagnosis' (denial). |
| 3. Stop bugging me. | Precontemplation | Expresses no need/desire for help (projection). |
| 4. I'm quite happy. | Precontemplation | Appears not distressed about the situation. |
| 5. I forgot etc. | Precontemplation | When failed to keep appointment with teacher. |
| 6. It's not me it's . . . | Precontemplation | External attribution of cause of the problem. |
| 7. All teachers are d***heads. | Precontemplation | External attribution of cause of the problem. |
| 8. Yes I do misbehave but so does everybody else. | Precontemplation/ Contemplation | Acknowledgement of the act but not of the problem. |
| 9. Everybody messes about. | Precontemplation | I'm no different from everybody else. |
| 10. If they (teachers) leave me alone I won't bother them. | Precontemplation | External attribution of the problem. |
| 11. I haven't got any problems. | Precontemplation | Denial of the problem situation. |
| 12. It's the teachers, they pick on me. | Precontemplation | External attribution. |
| 13. Sometimes I'm disruptive. | Contemplation | Accepts feed back about own behaviour. |

| 14. | I don't like getting in trouble. | Contemplation | Concern expressed about the situation. |
|---|---|---|---|
| 15. | Can I remain in school if I behave myself? | Contemplation | An example of 'envisioning'. |
| 16. | Sometimes I behave myself. | Contemplation | Implicit acknowledgement that pupil sometimes misbehaves. |
| 17. | Sometimes I do mess about. | Contemplation | Differs from 9 above as uses the 'I' self-reference pronoun – 'I' statements should be encouraged. |
| 18. | Perhaps I could behave better. | Contemplation | Acknowledging a problem may exist. |
| 19. | What can I do? | Contemplation/ Determinism | A wish to do something about the problem. The pupil is ready to consider moving into active change. |
| 20. | Yes, I would like to keep out of trouble. | Contemplation/ Determinism | Acknowledgement of the problem situation and a desire for change; falls short of a statement of intent to do something about problem but this may be implicit. |
| 21. | I counted to ten when I felt like swearing. | Determinism | An example of the pupil experimenting with self-change strategies. |
| 22. | What can I do? | Determinism | The decision for active change has been taken. |
| 23. | I don't care if they kick me out of school. | Determinism | Has expressed a reluctance to change and will accept the consequences. |
| 24. | Keeping this diary makes me think about changing my behaviour. I don't misbehave as much. | Active change | Self-change programme ongoing. |
| 25. | I'm aiming for good reports. | Active change | Self-motivated change target set. |
| 26. | I think I've got worse since I stopped keeping the diary | Relapse | The gains made during active change may have been lost. |

## CONCLUDING COMMENTS

Engaging clients in programmes to improve their situation requires that the client wants to change, i.e. is motivated. In many life contexts, including schools, clients are not motivated to change. Consequently if change is necessary either change has to be imposed, which may be a very difficult task, or else clients have to be provided with an opportunity to become motivated – and motivational interviewing allows the 'helper' to make available that opportunity.

Motivational interviewing is an optimistic approach to helping people change because it rejects the view that motivation is an aspect of personality and therefore substantially resistant to change. Rather, it views motivation in a practical manner and describes the concept in a manner which is useful. In other words, an individual's commitment or non-commitment to change in a problem area of functioning (e.g. alcohol or drug abuse) is viewed as the individual's motivation or non-motivation to change. Further, if the individual is helped to develop a desire for change then the individual can be said to have been helped to acquire motivation.

Motivational interviewing is being used in an increasing number of situations in which counselling help is offered. Apart from designated staff with significant pastoral responsibilities, it is unlikely that many teachers will engage in motivational interviewing in counselling situations – but most teachers with a knowledge of the theory and techniques of motivational interviewing can incorporate some of the techniques into their day to day conversations with pupils.

With training it may well be that in the future the behaviours that make up 'motivational interviewing' will become part and parcel of 'normal' teacher behaviour and thus contribute to an even more positive motivational milieu in our schools.

# References

Alessi, G. (1998) 'Direct Observation Methods for Emotional/Behavioural Problems: Behavioural Assessment in Schools', in E. S. Shapiro and T. R. Kratochwill (eds) New York and London: The Guilford Press.

Axelrod, R. (1977) *Behaviour Modification for the Classroom Teacher*. New York: McGraw-Hill Book Co.

Becker, W. C., Englemann, S., Thomas, D. R. (1975) *Classroom Management*. Henley-on Thames: Science Research Associates.

Boekaerts, M. (1994) *Motivation in Education*. The Fourteenth Vernon-Wall Lecture delivered at the Annual Conference of the Education Section of The British Psychological Society.

Chisholme, B. *et al.* (1986) *Preventive Approaches to Disruption*. Windsor: NFER/Nelson.

Covington, M. V. (1992) *Making the Grade: A Self-Worth Perspective on Motivation and School Reform*. Cambridge: Cambridge University Press.

DfE (1994) *Pupils with Problems*. Joint Circulars issued by the Department for Education and the Department of Health. Circular 8/94: Pupil Behaviour and Discipline.

DfEE (1994) *The Code of Practice on the Identification and Assessment of Special Educational Needs*. DFE Publication Centre, PO Box 2193, London E15 2EU.

DfEE (1998) *Draft Guidance on Home School Agreeements*. DfEE Publication Centre, PO Box 2193, London E15 2EU.

DiClemente, C. C. (1981) 'Self-Efficacy and Smoking Cessation Maintenance: A Preliminary Report', *Cognitive Therapy and Research* **5**, 175–87.

Duffy, V. (1992) 'Lunchtime relaxation classes for GCSE pupils, *Times Educational Supplement*, 12 June.

Galvin, P., Mercer, S., Costa, P. (1990) *Building a Better Behaved School*. Harlow: Longman.

Glasser, W. (1990) *The Quality School: Managing Students Without Coercion*. New York: Harper Collins.

Harrop, A. (1983) *Behaviour Modification in the Classroom*. London: Hodder and Stoughton.

HMSO (1989) *Discipline in Schools*: Report of the Committee of Enquiry Chaired by Lord Elton. London: Her Majesty's Stationery Office.

Jolly, M. and McNamara, E. (1992) *Assessment: Towards Better Behaviour*. TBB, 7 Quinton Close, Ainsdale, Merseyside PR8 2TD.

Jolly, M. and McNamara, E. (1994) *Towards Better Behaviour Part III (Intervention)*. TBB, 7 Quinton Close, Ainsdale, Merseyside PR8 2TD.

Kanfer, F. H. and Karoly, P. (1972) 'Self Control: a Behavourist's Excursion into the Lions Den', *Behaviour Therapy*, **3**, 398–416.

Levy, R. L. (1977) 'Relationship of an overt commitment to task compliance in behaviour therapy', *Journal of Behaviour Therapy and Experimental Psychiatry* **8**, 25–9.

Madsen, C., Becker, W. C., Thomas, D. R. (1968) 'Rules, praise and ignoring elements of elementary classroom control', *Journal of Applied Behaviour Analysis* **1**, 139–50.

McAllister, L. W. *et al.* (1969) 'The application of operant conditioning techniques in a Secondary school classroom', *Journal of Applied Behaviour Analysis* **2**, 277–85.

McNamara, E. (1985) 'Sanction and Incentive Systems in the Secondary School: A Survey Enquiry', *The Durham and Newcastle Research Review*, **55**, 31–46.

McNamara, E. (1986) 'The Effectiveness of Incentive and Sanction Systems used in Secondary Schools: A Behavioural Analysis', *The Durham and Newcastle Research Review*, **56**, 285–290.

McNamara, E. (1988a) 'The use of rules and evaluative statements to promote pupil on-task behaviour', *Behavioural Approaches With Children* **12**, 45–54.

McNamara, E. (1988b) The self-management of school phobia: a case study', *Behavioural Psychotherapy* **16**, 217–229.

McNamara, E. (1990) 'The prevention and management of troublesome behaviour: a problem solving model', *Positive Teaching* **I**(2), 81–7.

McNamara, E. (1998) 'Beyond behaviourism: the role of cognition', *Pastoral Care in Education*.

Miller, W. R. and Rollnick, S. (eds) (1991) *Motivational Interviewing: Preparing People to Change*. New York: The Guilford Press.

Ollendick, T. H. (1983) 'Reliability and validity of the Revised Fear Survey Schedule for Children', *Behaviour Research and Therapy* **21**, 685–692.

Patterson, G. R. and Reid, J. (1971) 'Reciprocity and coercion: two facets of social systems', in Neuringer, C. and Michael, J. (eds) *Behaviour Modification in Clinical Psychology*. New York: Appleton, Century and Crofts.

Prochaska, J. O. and DiClemente, C. C. (1982) *The Transtheoretical Approach: Crossing Traditional Boundaries of Therapy*. Homewood, Il: Dowe Jones/Irwin.

Reynolds, C. R. and Richmond, B. O. (1978) 'What I think and feel: a Revised Measure of Children's Manifest Anxiety Scale', *Journal of Abnormal Child Psychology* **6**, 271–80.

Stuart, R. B. (1969) 'Assessment of changes of the communicational patterns of juvenile delinquents and their families', in Rubin, R. D. (ed.) *Advances in Behaviour Therapy*. New York: Academic Press.

Stuart, R. B. (1971) 'Behavioural contracting within the families of delinquents', *Journal of Behaviour Therapy and Experimental Psychiatry* **2**, 1–11.

Van Bilsen, H. (1991) 'Motivational Interviewing: Perspectives from the Netherlands', in Miller, W. R. and Rollnick, S. (eds) *Motivational Interviewing: Preparing People to Change*. New York: The Guilford Press.

Wilson, P. (1996) *Mental Health in Your School: A Guide for Teachers and Others Working in Schools*. London: Jessica Kingsley Publications.

## FURTHER READING

Baker, R. (1995) *Understanding Panic Attacks and Overcoming Fear*. Oxford: Lion Publishing plc.

Edelmann, R. (1995) *Anxiety: Theory Research and Intervention in Clinical and Health Psychology*. Chichester: John Wiley and Sons.

Kennerley, H. (1995) *Managing Anxiety*. Oxford: Oxford University Press.

King, J. N., Hamilton, D. I., Ollendick, T. H. (1994) *Children's Phobias: a Behavioural Perspective*.

Winett, R. A. and Winkler, R. C. (1972) 'Current behaviour modification in the classroom: be still, be quiet, be docile', *Journal of Applied Behaviour Analysis*, **5**, 499–504.

# Index

Printed in the United Kingdom
by Lightning Source UK Ltd.
104043UKS00002B/267-274